浙江省博物馆

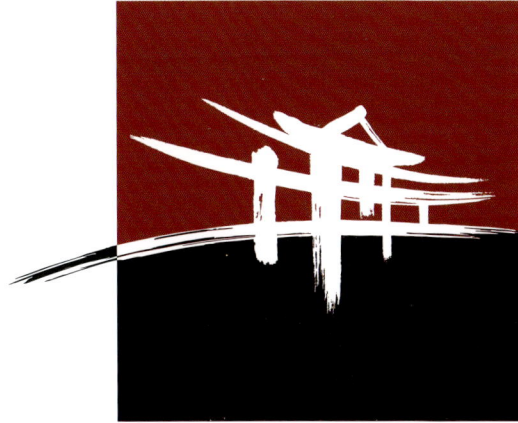

ZHEJIANG PROVINCIAL MUSEUM

浙江慈溪木艺堂藏历代竹雕精品（特集）编审委员会

主　　任：陈　浩

编　　委：王　炬　王屹峰　许洪流　陈　浩　陈　平　李　刚
　　　　　沈军甫　沈琼华　杨　铿　郑幼明　范佩玲　钟凤文
　　　　　赵幼强　梅丛笑　雍泰岳　蔡小辉　黎毓馨

策　　划：陈　平　王　炬

执行策划：钟凤文

浙江民间收藏精品走进博物馆系列特展之六

竹韵·浙江慈溪木艺堂藏历代竹雕精品

主办单位：浙江省博物馆

展览时间：2011年11月18日～2012年2月18日

展览地点：浙江省博物馆孤山馆区

展览策划：陈　平　钟凤文　郭永尧

展品选审：柴眩华　马争鸣　钟凤文　郭永尧

内容设计：陈　平　钟凤文　郭永尧

形式设计：王　炬　李卫平

特集撰文：柴眩华　钟凤文

英文翻译：徐雪英

竹韻

鮑賢倫

浙江民间收藏精品走进博物馆系列

# 竹 韻

## 浙江慈溪木艺堂藏历代竹雕精品

### Charm of Bamboo

Gems of Bamboo Engraving Articles Throughout History
Collected by Cixi Woodwork Hall, Zhejiang

浙江省博物馆 编

文物出版社

# 序

断竹，续竹，飞土，逐肉。

这是一首记载于《吴越春秋》中的上古歌谣——弹歌，再现了先民们取自然之竹，制作工具，猎取食物的场景，反映了上古时期先民已开始制作和使用竹制工具了，也是艺术源于生活之写照。

竹，在我国分布广泛，品种繁多，易种易得，质坚性韧，耐磨而不乏柔性，为先民们生产和生活常用之材，艺术之竹首先是生活之竹。以竹为器的早期遗存皆为实用之器，如：江苏常州圩墩新石器时代遗址出土的矛形竹器；浙江萧山跨湖桥遗址出土的距今8000年的竹篾编织制品，已经是稍微复杂的竹类制品了；湖北江陵战国楚墓出土的竹卮，融入了髹漆、彩绘等工艺，是高一级的复合工艺竹制品；湖南长沙马王堆西汉墓出土的竹勺，更是带透雕和浮雕工艺的高级竹雕器。至魏晋时期，竹器已涉及生产和生活的各个方面。晋人记载："广人以竹丝为布，甚柔美；蜀人以竹织履；可制篾编笆为篱笆；断材为柱，为栋，为舟楫，为桶斛，为弓矢，为笥、盒、杯，为箔、席、枕、几，为笙、簧乐器；实可服食，汁可疗病，笋可为蔬。其中恒多，莫可枚举。"虽然尚未胜数，但已涵盖了衣、食、住、行、兵、乐。结合墓葬出土实况，虽然文野有别，但从王侯将相至贩夫走卒都广泛使用物美易得的竹制品。

从晋代"竹林七贤"、王徽之"何可一日无此君"，到宋代苏东坡"宁可食无肉，不可居无竹。无肉令人瘦，无竹令人俗"，中国古代的文人士大夫正经历着将竹人格化的嬗变，其"刚、柔、忠、义"人格化的儒家美德渐渐地植入了文人的精神世界。特别是宋元之际，文人咏竹、写竹的名作辈出，如苏东坡的《于潜僧绿筠轩》，文与可的"文湖州竹派"。元代著名大画家如吴镇、柯九思、王蒙、王渊、顾安等都是写竹高手，所绘之竹均乃胸中之竹，各具风骨和情怀。这些名家大多生活或任职于环太湖流域的吴越之地，似乎在为这人文渊薮之地孕育中国独有的艺术门类——竹刻艺术品而铺垫艺术养分。

明代中期以后，富庶的江南特别是环太湖地区，已出现资本主义萌芽，封建的人身依附关系日渐松懈，许多能工巧匠通过折银摆脱匠籍的束缚，并以精湛的手艺来满足社会对"器用精巧"的需求，因而涌现出一大批引领行业的艺术大师，有些还是开山之祖，如紫砂壶龚春和时大彬、玉雕陆子冈、铜炉张鸣岐、牙角鲍天成、螺钿江千里、琢砚顾二娘等。如此的氛围，及周边竹文化的影响，中国最早的、也是影响最大的竹刻艺术流派——嘉定派在现上海的嘉定地区诞生了。其后的金陵派、希黄留青刻、芷岩浅刻等竹刻流派各树一帜，推波助澜，将中国古代竹刻艺术推向高峰。流派的出现，不是竹雕工艺的简单升级，而是从题材、表现形式到竹人全方位的艺术升华。从明晚期到清中期竹刻艺术黄金时期的知名竹人几乎都是美术家，他们自图自刻，将绘画原理运用于竹刻，以刀代笔，用刀痕表现笔墨趣味，竹子仅是他们书写艺术理想的载体，这一件件被赋予性灵的"薄技小器"，攒成了质朴、儒雅的竹刻艺术史，也铸就了竹刻艺术特有的文人气息和中国特色。

竹刻艺术品并非一日之功可为，成之不易，得之也不易，名家名作往往被藏之秘阁，市面流传甚少。郭永尧，宁波金鲁班大木作园林有限公司、香港贺升（宁波）建筑工程有限公司董事长，少年时即为生计而习木艺，由此痴迷上中国古代硬木家具，其收藏的黄花梨、紫檀木家具在收藏界口碑颇佳，多次为国有博物馆借展、交流。近十几年来，郭先生对古家具的姊妹艺术——竹刻器兴趣渐浓，陆续收藏竹刻器三百多件，其中既有涉及生活各个方面的精致器用，也有文人气息浓郁的典雅竹刻艺术品，其中不乏名家名作，从生活、生产、雅玩等各个层面展现明、清及民国竹器和竹艺之状况和发展。兹遴选其有代表性的竹刻器一百三十五件，编撰成《竹韵》一书付梓出版，以飨广大藏友和竹艺爱好者。同名展览也将于2011年11月中旬在浙江省博物馆孤山馆区与广大观众见面，这是我馆整合利用民间收藏的文物资源，让社会公众共享的再次实践。

浙江省博物馆馆长 陈浩

2011年10月

# Preface

Felling and breaking bamboo, making slingshots with cut bamboo, shooting pellets with slingshots, hunters getting food.

This is an ancient poem in *Spring and Autumn of States Wu and Yue*, which shows our forefathers' hunting for food. Beside, it manifests that our forefathers began to make and use bamboo tools, a true representation that art is originated in life.

Bamboo, widely distributed in China with a great variety, easy accessibility, fine quality, tenacity, wear-resistance and flexibility, was used by our forefathers for their life and production. Bamboo of art was originated in the bamboo for life and it was best demonstrated in the early remains, e.g. spear-shaped bamboo articles in Weidun Neolithic Age Remains in Changzhou, Jiangsu; articles woven by bamboo strips unearthed in Kuahuqiao Remains in Xiaoshan, Zhejiang about 8000 years ago, which were complicated bamboo products; bamboo cups unearthed from the Tomb of the Chu State, the Warring States Period in Jiangling, Hubei, which were composite bamboo works of art integrating lacquer and color painting craftsmanship; the bamboo ladle unearthed from Mawangdui Western Han Tomb in Changsha, Hunan, which were advanced bamboo articles with openwork and relief engraving. In addition, the bamboo articles were widely applied in the life and production in the Wei and Jin Periods. It was recorded in the Jin Dynasty that "People of Guang weave soft and beautiful cloth with bamboo silk; people of Shu make shoes with bamboo; bamboo strips can be used as fences; bamboo can be used as columns, beams, ships, barrels, measure, bows, arrows, baskets, boxes, cups, screens, mats, pillows, tea tables and musical instruments. Moreover, bamboo shoots can be consumed as food, juice as medicine, which are really numerous to number." To sum up, the bamboo covers different aspects of our life: food, clothing, transportation, shelter, military and entertainment. Judging from the archeological discoveries, not only kings, lords, generals and tradesmen, but also porters, peddlers and menial servants all enjoyed the bamboo products.

On the other hand, ancient Chinese literati and officials personified bamboo to a great extent and the Confucianistic virtues of "strength, softness, loyalty and justice" embodied in the bamboo were gradually transplanted into the spiritual world of ancient men of letters, for example, there appeared "Seven worthy people in the bamboo forest" and "How can one live without bamboo?" by Wang Huizhi in the Jin Dynasty, and Su Dongpo of the Song Dynasty once said, "It's better to have food without meat than have a residence without bamboo. We become thin without meat, but we become vulgar without bamboo." Moreover, in the Song and Yuan Dynasties, there appeared a lot of famous works praising bamboo, such as "Yuqian Monk: Green Pavilion" by Su Dongpo; "Huzhou Bamboo School" of Wen Yuke. And in the Yuan Dynasty, many famous painters, e.g. Wu Zhen, Ke Jiusi, Wang Meng, Wang Yuan and Gu An were all distinguished painters of bamboo with different atmosphere and dispositions. These masters once lived or worked in the land of Wu and Yue around Taihu Lake Basin, which nurtured the prosperity of bamboo works of art, a unique art in China.

After the mid-Ming Dynasty, with burgeoning capitalism in the affluent Jiangnan area, in particular, in Pan-Taihu Lake area, many skillful craftsmen, through buying their freedom, were freed from the craftsmanship registration and satisfied the social needs for "delicate articles" with their superb skills, therefore, a group of leading masters of art was sprouting, and some were pioneers in their trade, e.g. Gong Chun's and Shi Dabin's red enameled pottery, Lu Zigang's jade carving, Zhang Mingqi's copper incense burners, Bao Tiancheng's ivory and rhinoceros horn engraving, Jiang Qianli's mother-of-pearl inlaying and Gu Erniang's ink stone making. Under the influence of such a trend and surrounding bamboo culture, Jiading School—the earliest and biggest bamboo engraving school was born in Jiading, Shanghai. Subsequently, Jinling School, Xihuang's flat engraving, Zhiyan's shallow engraving formed different schools, pushing the ancient Chinese bamboo art to the summit, since different schools embodied the artistic sublimation of themes, expressions and bamboo engravers instead of the simple upgrading of bamboo engraving skills. Famous bamboo engravers during the golden period from the late Ming to the mid Qing Dynasties were also artists, who integrated painting with bamboo engraving and expressed the flavor of brush pens in bamboo engraving with their knives. Bamboo, as a carrier to express their artistic ideas, became "a small article of craftsmanship" endowed with a soul, which not only depicted the history of bamboo engraving with simplicity and elegance, but helped forge the unique literati atmosphere and Chinese characteristics prevalent in bamboo engraving.

Famous bamboo engraving works are often collected and stored in private since they are not easy to be made and obtained. Guo Yongyao, president of Ningbo Golden Lu Ban Woodwork Gardening Co., Ltd. and Hesheng (Ningbo) Construction Project Co., Ltd. Hong Kong, learned carpentry for a living in his early years and then began to be obsessed with ancient Chinese hardwood furniture, especially, the yellow rosewood and rosewood furniture collected by him enjoyed high reputation in the collection circle and were once on loan to the state-owned museums. In the past decades, with a strong interest in bamboo engraving articles, Mr. Guo has collected over 300 articles, including delicate articles for daily use and elegant works of art with aromatic literati atmosphere, some of which are articles by renowned artists and they show the development of bamboo articles and bamboo engraving art of the Ming and Qing Dynasties and the Republic of China for life, production and appreciation. Selected here are 136 bamboo articles and the book *Charm of Bamboo—Gems of Bamboo Engraving Articles Throughout History Collected by Cixi Woodwork Hall, Zhejiang* is to be published for the delight of collectors and bamboo art lovers. Moreover, the exhibition of the same name is to be held in Gushan Branch, Zhejiang Provincial Museum in November, which is an endeavor of ZPM in making use of the folk cultural relic resources and in serving the general public.

Chen Hao

Curator of Zhejiang Provincial Museum

October 2011

# 绿竹猗猗　尚象成形

## ——古代竹刻艺术及识辨

竹子节实竿挺，四季常青，自古以来被视作祥瑞之物，其虚心劲节、弯而不屈的品质，又被认为具有"君子"之风，历来受到世人特别是文人的喜爱，几千年来一直为文人墨客吟咏、歌颂。《诗经》中就有"瞻彼其奥，绿竹猗猗"的赞美。宋代以来，文人们颂竹、咏竹、写竹、画竹不断，涌现了无数的名篇佳作，苏东坡"宁可食无肉，不可居无竹"成千古之唱。在长期接触过程中，人们认识到了竹子在日常生活中的用途，依据考古发掘材料，我国用竹的历史可上溯到新石器时代。古代竹制品的大量使用，给竹刻艺术创造了物质条件。明以前传世的竹刻器物和知名刻工较少，自明中叶正德、嘉靖以后到清代，竹刻名家辈出，使竹刻艺术从实用为主转变成为供人们鉴赏收藏的艺术品，从而使竹刻艺术成为专门的工艺美术门类。竹刻艺术家们以刀代笔，以竹子为载体，将书、画、诗、印等艺术形式融为一体，赋予竹子以新的生命。他们的努力，为中国竹文化的发展与繁荣，作出了重大贡献。竹刻艺术是中国工艺美术史上一朵淡雅的奇葩，也是人类历史的文化遗产。本文拟从竹刻的时代风格、工艺技法、常见器形和价值评定几方面，扼要介绍古代竹刻艺术品的断代与辨伪。

## 一、竹刻的分期与艺术风格

据文献和实物遗存的情况来看，竹刻艺术的发展大致可分为明代以前、明代、清代前期、清代后期和民国时期几个阶段。不同时期，各有其时代风格。

### （一）明代以前

竹刻起源历史悠久，由于历史和自然环境等因素，竹器很难保存，故传世甚少。近年在考古发掘中，发现了不少早期的竹器，有用于记载文字的竹简，有日常生活的器具。2002年浙江杭州萧山跨湖桥遗址出土一件距今8000年属于跨湖桥文化的竹篾席状编织物，该编织物形状呈梯形，三面残，完整一面斜向收边，较宽一侧有T字相交的木质条骨编织其中，是迄今为止中国已知的最早的竹制品[①]。浙江湖州地区钱山漾遗址出土了距今大约5000年良渚文化时期的竹编物二百多件，有竹席、篓、篮等，特别是其中采用的像"梅花眼"、"辫子口"这些较为复杂的编织花式，没有相当的技术水平是不能运用自如的[②]。这些为古人使用竹器提供了实物的例证。

战国秦汉时期，漆器盛行，漆雕艺术繁荣，漆器的器胎，有相当一部分是用竹片制成的，受漆雕艺术的影响，后来竹器本身的制作也萌生了艺术化的倾向。湖北江陵战国楚墓出土竹卮3件，均用圆筒形竹节雕成器身，另加竹盖，全器髹黑漆或朱漆彩绘[③]。湖南长沙马王堆一号西汉墓出土采用透雕和浮雕两种技法的龙纹彩漆竹勺2件[④]。甘肃武威汉墓出土2件竹笔管，中部隶书阴刻"白马作"、"史虎作"[⑤]。这几件考古出土文物，是今天我们研究竹刻史的珍贵资料，它有力证明，至迟在战国时期，手工匠们就已懂得采用竹子这种常见材料进行雕刻。

南北朝时期，据《南齐书·明僧绍传》记载，齐高帝曾将一件竹根雕成的如意"笋箨冠"赏赐给当时的大隐士明僧绍。北周文学家庾信《奉报赵王惠酒》诗中也有"野炉然树叶，山杯捧竹根。"即用竹根雕制成的酒杯。这些都是竹工艺品，而有别于一般器用。

竹刻成为一种艺术品种，当在唐宋之间，但传世极少。这一时期的竹刻制品已经非常精美，而且雕刻工艺也日趋完善，已具备各种不同技法。目前可见传世最早的竹刻实物，为藏于日本奈良正仓院的一件唐代竹雕留青人物花鸟纹尺八，长43.6厘米，采用留青刻法，施阴文浅雕仕女、树木、花草、禽蝶等图案，刻工极为精致，与当时金银器镂錾及石刻线雕相似。另据宋人郭若虚《图画见闻志》记载：唐时德州刺史王倚家有一竹笔管，"刻《从军行》一铺，人马毛发，亭台云水，无不精绝。每一事刻《从军行》诗两句，……似非人功，其画迹若粉描，向明方可辨之。"可知这是浅刻毛雕法。元代陶宗仪《辍耕录》中记载了宋高宗时期竹刻家詹成擅制鸟笼，"四面花版，皆于竹片上刻成宫室、人物、山水、花木、禽鸟，纤悉俱备，其细若缕，且玲珑活动。"这是透雕技法。詹成也是竹刻艺术史上见诸文献记载最早的一位艺人。宁夏银川西夏八号陵出土一竹雕人物残片，残长7厘米、宽2.7厘米，以卷草及方格锦纹等作地，上刻人物，背景为庭院、松树、假山[6]。此残件是目前为止南宋竹刻的唯一标本。尽管如此，当时的竹刻仍然只是一种工艺手段，更多地运用到器物的装饰上，单独的竹刻制品极为少见，传世器物及知名刻工绝少，文献记载亦鲜，似尚未形成专门艺术。

## （二）明代

竹刻真正发展成为一种专门艺术是在明中期以后，喜好刻竹的文人雅士自己画稿、设计，并亲自奏刀，"随后或父子相传，或师徒授受，或私下仿效，习之者众，遂成专业。"清嘉庆年间，嘉定人金元钰著《竹人录》，根据不同的地域和雕刻技法，分为金陵（今南京）和嘉定（今属上海）两派。金陵派尚简洁，以浅刻为主，作品重线条，笔划有致，韵味古雅，流行竹刻扇骨。嘉定派尚细工，以透雕、深雕、高浮雕为主，写实功夫独创，作品精致而雅小，凡山水、人物、鸟兽及楼阁皆求写实与奇特，制器初为簪钗等饰品，后逐渐为几案间陈置器物所取代，盛行竹刻笔筒、笔搁、诗筒、棋盒等。

嘉定派竹刻创始人为朱鹤（字子鸣，号松邻，主要活动于嘉靖至万历时期），与其子朱缨（字清甫，号小松，1520～1587年）、其孙朱稚征（号三松，1570～1650年）祖孙三代被誉为"嘉定三朱"。朱氏三代刻竹，取材广泛，早期雕刻刀法以纤巧工谨见长，其后稍有变化，追求繁简适度的艺术效果，至三松时，更臻完善，达到以刀代笔的境界，曾有"小松出而名掩松邻，三松出而名掩小松"之说。三朱作品以"深刀刻法，即奏刀深峻，洼隆浅深，可五六层"为主要特征，表现出丰富的画面层次及立体效果，其山水人物追寻简朴古拙、异趣横生之北宗风格，而花鸟则多仿徐熙的清淡典雅之意境，开创了明代以来刻竹结合绘画技法之先河，对后世竹木雕刻产生了巨大影响。

推为金陵派刻竹开山的濮仲谦，复姓濮阳，单称姓濮，名澄，字仲谦，南京人，生于万历十年（1582年），清初尚健在。他刻竹的特点通常是以浅刻为主，并且又善于选材，最喜用盘根错节的竹根或焦竹，根据原料的自然形状和特征，往往刻划数刀，即将其制成一件精巧的艺术品。《太平府志》中记载他"有巧思，以镂刻名世，一切犀玉竹皿器，经其手即古雅可爱。"据记载，濮仲谦所制水磨竹器像扇骨、酒杯、笔筒、笔搁之类，也都

妙绝一时，他还能制紫檀、乌木、象牙等器，但不多见。濮仲谦名声在当时极大，真迹传世极罕，赝品特多，大凡雕工繁琐而题材庸俗的，多系后人伪刻，有的取无款旧器妄添濮氏之名。

除嘉定和金陵两大流派外，还有一位堪称巨匠、被誉为"留青圣手"的张希黄，本名宗略，字希黄，传江苏江阴或浙江嘉兴人，活跃于明朝末年，他善用留青的技法来浅浮雕山水亭台的景色，而且屋宇、树石、人物皆细微精致，可惜作品流传甚少。从记载与实物看，张希黄的作品基本上以远景山水、亭台楼阁、园林人物为题材，楼阁多是些水边建筑，如水榭、望江楼等等，这些建筑刻划工细规整，类似绘画中的界画。人物在画面中往往只起点缀作用，一般仅一厘米高，人物神情完全靠身体姿态来表现。又常喜爱在构景的留白部分刻上数行诗句，留青的行楷体，笔法酣畅，再加印款，使诗句与画景联结，虽为竹刻，却如一幅小小的书画作品。

朱氏的透雕、深雕和高浮雕，濮氏的浅刻兼略施刀凿，张氏的留青浅刻，形成为明代竹刻的三大风格。

（三）清代前期

自清初至乾隆为清前期，这是竹刻艺术的黄金时期。无论在装饰题材还是雕刻技巧方面，都比明晚期更呈多元化，总体艺术风格仍承袭明代朱氏高浮雕、透雕的传统，有的在继承之余加深造诣，探索雕刻之奥妙，推陈出新。艺术家们糅合了多种雕刻技法，创造出许多生动活泼、丰富多彩的作品，诸如"竹林七贤"、"对弈图"、"听松图"、"观瀑图"、"赤壁图"等反映文人雅士的生活情趣，寓意"吉祥"、"万年如意"、"八仙祝寿"等题材的作品大量涌现，一反前人深厚朴实的风格，而以新奇见长，构图虽简单，造型却极佳，雕刻也十分精细，所有边棱部分都很圆滑，对器顶、器背以及底部均着意处理。器形较明代丰富，多见有诗筒、笔筒、香筒、臂搁、墨床、笔洗、人物、仙佛、螃蟹、蟾蜍等等，此外，这一时期复古思想盛行，竹刻艺术中的仿古制品也相继出现，如仿古竹鼎、竹瓶、竹壶等。此时名家辈出，吴之璠微妙入神的薄地阳文、封氏兄弟的立体圆雕、周颢的南宗山水和陷地深刻以及潘西凤兼工浅雕深刻的技艺，皆冠绝当时，无出其右，将中国的竹刻艺术推向鼎盛。

吴之璠，字鲁珍，号东海道人，江苏嘉定人，生卒年不详，工人物、花鸟、行草，尤善竹刻，刻竹年款多在康熙前期，是三松之后的第一高手，当时文人学者对他的竹刻艺术有很高的称誉，作品也曾贡入内府。吴之璠擅长多种刻法，除立体圆雕外，更善浮雕，他的浮雕有两种：一种继承三朱的刻法但又有所发展，以深刻作高浮雕，深浅多层，高凸出接近圆雕，低陷处或用透雕。另一种是减地浮雕法，介于朱氏高浮雕与浅浮雕之间，是摹拟龙门石刻中的浅浮雕技艺而自出新意的刻法，为前人所未备，《竹人录》作者金元钰以"薄地阳文"名之，成为吴氏浅浮雕刻法之术语。他常常以浅浮雕来突出主题，留空四周作为背景，刻划只占全器某一局部之一事一物，其余部分则用去地法刮至露出竹的纹理，任其光素，即使有所雕刻，也不过略加勾勒而已。吴之璠传世之作尚多，康雍之际也曾形成一个以吴之璠为首的竹刻流派——薄地阳文派，类似刻法作品，传至后世也不少。

以立体圆雕为代表的封氏家族，是嘉定的竹刻世家，子孙世代相传至咸丰、同治年间，都是竹刻名手，其中尤以康熙时封锡爵（字晋侯）、封锡禄（字义侯，晚号廉痴）、

封锡璋（字汉侯）兄弟最为著名，号称竹刻鼎足。康熙四十二年（1703年），锡禄、锡璋同时被召入京城，供奉养心殿，一时名扬各地，竹刻艺人服务于宫廷也自此开始。封氏兄弟主要是继承明晚期朱氏的风格，而尤精于圆雕，其作品多以新奇造型见胜，他们以竹根为原料，创作雕刻民间喜爱的人物如"刘海戏蟾"、"布袋和尚"之类。其雕刻技巧不像朱氏的古拙，而是用刀运腕如风，镂雕圆浑精湛，细入毫发，所刻人物的手足位置、衣服纹理、面目神情，尤其是老者鸡皮鹤发，胁肋之骨，结喉露齿，均生动自然，超愈前人。可惜真迹流传甚少，或许由于后人过于注重三朱之名，封氏作品款识常遭剜剔，另镌赝款，伪托三朱之制。

周芷岩是清代雍正至乾隆年间极负盛名的竹刻家，其名颢（一作灏），字晋瞻，号芷岩，又号雪樵、尧峰山人，晚号犉痴，江苏嘉定人（今上海），生于康熙二十四年（1685年），卒于乾隆三十八年（1717年）。他工行草，能诗画，最喜画竹，尤擅刻竹，不仅名载《竹人录》，《墨香居画识》、《墨林今话》等画籍中也有他的小传，如果说三朱以来竹刻家是竹人兼画师，那么周芷岩是画师兼竹人。周芷岩擅长以多种刀法刻各种题材，而最为人所称道的是他所刻山水。雍乾时期，"四王"南宗风靡画坛，芷岩破除以往竹刻山水崇尚北宗画法的传统，以南宗画法直接刻竹而别树一帜。用刀如用笔，不假画稿，自然流畅，其皴法浓淡坳突，生动浑成，所刻山水，人无耳目，屋无窗棂，树无细点，都为他人所不及。刀法一般多为阴刻，轮廓皴擦，多以一刀剜出，阔狭浅深，长短斜整，无不如意，树木枝干，以钝锋一剔而就，刀痕爽利。在竹刻史中，周芷岩是一位关键人物，竹雕风格至清中期转而一变，从其作品中可见一斑，他继承了嘉定竹刻的优良传统，而又能推陈出新，对后世有重大影响。

潘西凤是活跃于乾隆时期的竹刻家，字桐冈，号老桐，浙江新昌人，后来侨寓扬州，又因郑板桥称誉为濮仲谦之后第一人，所以一般将他看作金陵派。潘西凤精擅浅刻技法，所作多是简简数笔，却是线条柔勒有力，连绵不断，并且多以当时名家画本为构图，辅以题铭及印章。在臂搁上浅刻菊花极精。老桐所制器物略加刮削打磨而成，以不假人工刀斧为奇。

（四）清代后期

自嘉庆至宣统为清后期，以整个竹刻界来讲，无论制作工艺，还是设计构思，逐渐退化。这一时期刻竹的风格渐趋浅刻和平刻，镂空雕法与圆雕技法不再被普遍使用。竹刻家多不是文人出身，不能自画自刻，只能求画家设计打稿，竹人渐渐沦落成有如一般作坊内的刻工，往往只求笔情墨趣的相似，不求刀痕凿迹的精工。清后期的竹刻家虽多有记载，其间也有若干名家，如擅浅浮雕山水兼工刻小楷的王恒（字梅邻、仲文、茂林，号梅邻山人，生活于清嘉庆、道光年间）、工人物肖像的方絜（1800～1838年，字矩平，号治庵，浙江黄岩人）等等，但"自具面目，堪称大家的实罕其人。"当时画坛上正流行海上画派，往往以前人故事、戏剧人物、传说故事为题材，竹刻家自然也受到这种习尚的影响，竹刻图案题材大部分采用各家书画，力求以刀痕表现书画之笔墨，摹刻的书画，达到使人一望便知为某家笔法的地步，代表性人物是擅长画本的蔡照（原名照初，字容庄，浙江萧山人，活跃于咸丰、同治年间），常常与同乡任熊合作创制版画和竹器，他曾为萧山王龄（延居）刻扇骨一百柄，山水、花卉、仕女、佛像各种俱备，都由任渭长落墨，由其奏刀，刻法以阴文为主，借用刻刀在竹子上完美地再现了任熊绘画的笔墨意趣，传书画之神，极负盛名。同时由于金石学的盛兴，雕刻在竹器上的书法和铭文多以金石碑拓为主，或集款识，或拓器形，缩写钩摹，为前期所罕有，以技法言，各种糙地，都见用于此时，有砂地、核桃地、橘皮地种种名称。器形上除传统品种外，新出现旱烟筒杆、竹根酒杯、帽筒、围棋筒、镜盒、香烟盒、图章盒、贴簧扇等。

（五）民国时期

从整体上看，民国时期的竹刻已逐渐衰落，竹刻诸法也几近失传，这当中尽管也出现过一些知名的竹刻家，如时大经、谭维德、王杰人、张志鱼、龚玉璋、潘行庸、金绍堂、金绍坊和支慈庵等，但依然挽救不了它的颓势。这时的竹刻家大都缺少才情，既不善诗文，又不善书画，只凭摹仿他人的作品进行雕制，匠气明显的作品急剧增多。以文人书画家为主导的艺术创作，由主流变为支流，求简追易，作品往往给人以平浅单一的感觉。流行的竹刻器多为笔筒、臂搁、扇骨、名片盒、印章、旱烟筒杆、香烟嘴、眼镜盒、竹杖等等小件。

## 二、竹刻工艺技法

竹子的刻法大致有圆雕、阴刻、浮雕三大类，其中又可细分为毛雕、浅刻、深刻和浅浮雕、高浮雕、透雕、留青等若干小类（见下表）。

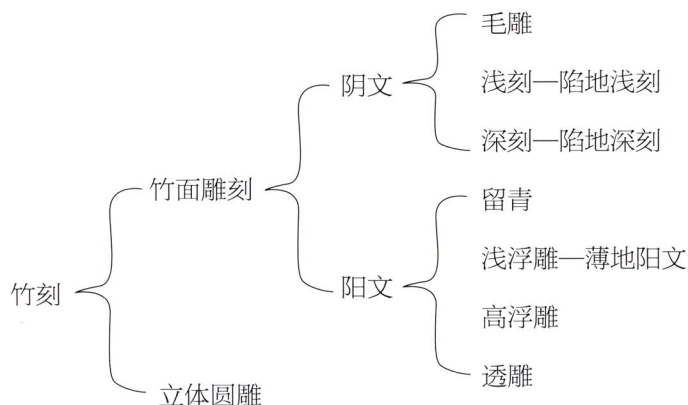

竹刻
- 竹面雕刻
  - 阴文
    - 毛雕
    - 浅刻—陷地浅刻
    - 深刻—陷地深刻
  - 阳文
    - 留青
    - 浅浮雕—薄地阳文
    - 高浮雕
    - 透雕
- 立体圆雕

竹雕大体上有这些刻法，并不是指一件器物只有某一种刻法，因为一件竹雕往往采用两种乃至多种刻法，但以某一种刻法为主还是看得出来的。不同竹刻工艺技法的出现在时代上有先后，这也是我们对竹刻作品断代的依据之一。在此，重点介绍竹刻的几种独特工艺技法如下。

陷地深刻：属深刻技法，竹材表面光素称为地，所雕图案全部刻陷于"地"中，最多至五六层，故名。此法始于清前期，乾嘉以后少用。

留青：又名皮雕。留青技法是留下需用的竹青雕刻图案，然后将其余部分的竹青薄薄地刮去，露出竹肌，竹青细滑如玉，竹肌有丝纹，竹青颜色浅，年数多了呈微黄，竹肌年愈久，色愈深，利用竹青与竹肌两者在质理、色泽上的差异对比，达成浮现主题的效果。凡用留青的竹皮，不能有丝毫的伤损，刻成才能莹洁如玉，善于留青的名家，常能以刀法在薄薄的青皮雕刻中产生许多变化，因为青筠可以有全留、少留、多留的差别，留得越少

越薄，竹肌的颜色越外泛，如琥珀之色，所以籍者多留少留，产生层次、浓淡之感，用以浅雕山水花鸟景色时，宛然如墨分五色。留青竹刻始于唐代，但唐以后有关留青竹雕的记载与实物均中断，直到明末竹刻家张希黄以此技见长于艺坛，现传世作品基本上为清以后的产品。

薄地阳文：就是将图案以外的全部竹地或邻近图案四周之竹地刮去，使图案微微高起，然后再细部雕刻于其上，属浅浮雕的一种。首创于清康熙吴之璠。

竹刻地纹：一为光地，即平地；二为空地，即透雕之镂空；三为几何纹地，如雷纹、波纹、鳞纹、锦纹等；四为糙地，即砂地，属阳纹刻法，地作砂粒状，名称有细纱地、粗砂地、核桃地、橘皮纹等。糙地出现在清道光时期。

贴黄：又称"竹黄"、"文竹"、"翻黄"，竹刻中的一种特殊工艺。是将竹材里层薄薄的竹黄翻转过来，经煮、压后贴在木胎上，然后加以雕饰。木胎多用黄杨木，因其色与竹黄接近。贴黄工艺产生在清初，创始于湖南邵阳地区，乾隆、嘉庆年间最为兴盛，在宫廷中广泛使用，后江苏嘉定、浙江黄岩、四川江安、福建上杭等地均有制作。

### 三、竹刻常见器形

严格地说，竹刻应分为竹根雕刻和竹茎雕刻两大类。

**（一）竹根雕**

竹根雕的选材，多注重于竹根外表的奇特，多有瘤节，是因其本身就具有古雅之风的缘故。竹根雕一般不多作处理，截取盘根错节的竹根后，根据其天然形态，进行构思创作，略加雕琢而成器。竹根雕作品，基本上都是供人玩赏的工艺摆件，艺术品位较高，常见的有神仙人物、飞禽走兽、山水小景、果蔬花卉、器物摹仿、笔洗笔架等。值得一提的是竹根仿犀角杯和竹根印章。

仿犀角杯：晚明清初流行犀角杯，因此，清初以竹根仿制犀角杯形器颇为盛行，大多以松树为主要纹饰，另附加鹤、鹿、松鼠，其他如人物、梅花、竹叶等纹饰，亦偶有所见，但不为多。清初流行的古松纹仿犀角杯，多为观赏之用，以岁寒三友、鹤鹿同春之类较为高雅题材，最受文人欢迎。康熙以后，该类仿犀角杯基本不再制作。

印章：竹根印章就竹根长势，雕成印钮，然后在印钮下方的平底刻篆文。用竹根篆刻印章始于清代。

**（二）竹茎雕**

竹茎雕刻种类繁多，若需做成圆形器物的，如笔筒、香筒等，则将竹节的部分截下来，或留其中一横槅，然后在其周身雕刻图案纹饰；如做臂搁、扇骨之类，则将竹筒从中剖开，然后成器。

竹茎雕常见器型主要有：

笔筒：用于毛笔存放的文房用具。外表多以书画雕刻作为装饰，因此又被广泛用作书房书案的工艺陈设。明代以前，搁笔多用"笔山"、"笔床"，直至明晚期，才有大量笔筒出现，早期笔筒以光素为主，不尚雕工。万历以后，竹刻笔筒体形渐大，选材亦渐厚；雕刻风格由光素转为浅浮雕，由浅浮雕转为高浮雕，再由高浮雕变为镂空雕，露出主题景物，达至圆雕效果。这种透雕笔筒为明晚期竹刻的一个特色。清代早期开始流

行"薄地阳文",透雕笔筒甚少出现。清代中期,笔筒体形更大,有的直径达20厘米以上,而且刻工较深。清代晚期体形又渐缩小,而雕刻以浅浮雕或阴刻为主。清末光绪、宣统间,留青笔筒大量出现。

香筒:专为熏香而作,又名香熏。是一镂空竹管,上下镶有木盖,为明代至清中期常见器物。明代香筒,题材以螭龙纹为多。清初香筒纹饰题材以民间故事为主,富民间生活气息。雍正以后,香筒刻工力求繁密精巧,雕刻景物层次渐多,至乾隆年间最为精美。清代晚期香筒可能为香炉所代替,几乎不见。

臂搁:又称"秘阁",文人临书枕臂的器具,用于书写时搁着手臂,免沾字墨。常作"覆瓦"形,两边平直,正面雕有丰富的书法、绘画图案,既作为文房用具,又是别具欣赏价值的艺术品。长期以来,一直为文人雅士所钟爱。明代竹刻臂搁,大部分为素工,存世甚少;清代臂搁,背面光素,直到清末民初,才出现背面刻纹的竹臂搁。

镇纸:一般多作尺形,又称"镇尺",用于压纸。作为尺形镇纸,多刻有兰、竹及双螭等纹饰,也有做成各种仿生造型的,但底部均平整。

盒子:用于盛放书册、笺纸、墨锭、印章、砚台的各类竹盒,有方形和圆形,带盖。这类竹盒,器表都雕镂各种纹饰,有的还镶嵌宝玉石、螺钿等,盒盖上往往刻有精美的书画。

扇骨:传统折扇的骨架,用以支撑扇面。扇骨的雕刻多采用留青技法,表面雕刻各种纹饰。

陈设件:明代竹雕陈设以仙佛造像为多,清代以后品种较为丰富,有佛手、如意、山子、荷蟹、蟾蜍、动物、果子等等,式样繁多。明代和清代早期人物、动物形象,其眼珠多嵌犀角或紫檀,清代后期以料珠替代。乾隆一朝宫中制作竹刻仿古铜器陈设用具甚多,有尊、匜、卣、壶、鼎、觚、瓶等等,不论造型还是纹饰,都模仿夏商周三代古青铜器而雕制,做工精巧绝伦,纤巧华丽,极具艺术观赏价值。

除上述器形之外,还有诗筒、信筒、花插、冠架、鸟笼、笔洗、笔管、鼻烟壶、香坠等等。

## 四、竹刻艺术品的价值评定

精美的竹刻不仅具有可以欣赏的艺术价值,而且具有较高的历史价值和经济价值,深受人们的青睐,作为一种艺术品,一般认为有以下几方面的品评标准:

第一,雕琢工艺。雕琢的价值不在细而在于工,不在俗而在于雅。竹雕突破面积狭小的竹材限制,通过竹刻家的神妙刻画,缩影活跃于方寸之间。一件好的竹刻器物,在雕工上往往借多种刻法以求变化,笔调单一易板滞,刀工变幻则神奇,在布局上疏中求疏,密中求密,疏而不空,密而不塞,虚实、宾主、阴阳向背各得其宜,因此刻竹以自家立意构思,自己打稿落墨,自己操刀运凿,书画皆出于一手为佳。

第二,款识。有款比无款好,有名家款识则更佳,当然也不能排除无款印或有而名姓不彰,艺术价值又颇高的作品,更何况名家款识还有真伪识别的问题。刻竹作伪方式和书画一样,大致有摹刻、仿刻、添款、臆造等四种方式,特别是摹拟名家的刀法而且刻上名家的姓名,或是将不具名的旧作品补刻上名家款识,有的刻工也极精巧,往往容

易鱼目混珠。

第三，年代。因竹刻件不易保存，故年代愈久，相对价值就越高，鉴别年代久远的标准主要看皮色红润的深浅而定，竹制作品表面色泽很丰富，有浅黄、棕黄、棕红、暗红、深棕等色，一般来说，深者年代久，浅者近，以色红如樱桃、如琥珀者为上品，黑色者为下品。清初作品往往具有一种灰褐色泽，而明代作品则多带有暗红色。

第四，件品。包括形制、大小及保存完善程度等。

以上几项条件都是相互联系的，只有经过综合评估，才能确定一件器物的价值及收藏与否。

柴旸华

## 注 释

① 浙江省文物考古研究所、萧山博物馆：《浦阳江流域考古报告之一——跨湖桥》文物出版社2004 年。

② 浙江省文物管理委员会：《吴兴钱山漾遗址第一、二次发掘报告》，《考古学报》1960 年第 2 期。

③ 湖北省博物馆、荆州地区博物馆、江陵县文物工作小组：《湖北江陵拍马山楚墓发掘简报》，《考古》1973 年第 3 期。

④ 《长沙马王堆一号汉墓》，文物出版社，1973 年。

⑤ 甘肃省博物馆、甘肃省武威县文化馆：《武威磨嘴子三座汉墓发掘简报》，《文物》1972 年第12 期。

⑥ 宁夏回族自治区博物馆：《西夏八号陵发掘简报》，《文物》1978 年第 8 期。

## 参考著录

① 王世襄编著：《竹刻》，人民美术出版社，1992 年。

② 叶义、谭志成：《中国竹刻艺术》，香港艺术馆，1982 年。

③ 李军：《明清竹刻》，宁波出版社，2005 年。

④ 赫崇政、成昭平、蔡国声：《竹木牙雕》，上海文化出版社，2002 年。

⑤ 《雕刻之珍——明清竹刻精选》，台北历史博物馆，2005 年。

# Slender Green Bamboo　Natural Forming of Appearance

## —Ancient Bamboo Engraving Art and Its Appreciation

Bamboo, with its straight and green nature, has long been held as an object of auspiciousness, and with its modesty and tenacity, it is adored and eulogized by the people, especially, the men of letters throughout history, to have an air of "gentleman". In *Book of Songs*, it was lauded as slender green bamboo. Since the Song Dynasty, a lot of songs, poems, essays and paintings eulogizing the bamboo have been created and the poetic lines of "It's better to have food without meat than have a residence without bamboo" by Su Dongpo has been popular till now. Beside, people have fully realized the practical use of bamboo. The history of using bamboo can date back to the Neolithic Age according to archeological discoveries. And the large-scale use of bamboo products nurtured the bamboo engraving art, especially, emerging generations of bamboo engraving masters from Reign Zhengde and Reign Jiajing of the mid Ming Dynasty to the Qing Dynasty pushed the bamboo engraving from the practical use to the works of art appreciated and collected by people and thus, bamboo engraving became a new category of art. Bamboo artists, with their knives, infused a new life into the bamboo by integrating calligraphy, painting, poems and seals, making a contribution to the development and prosperity of Chinese bamboo culture. Bamboo engraving is not only a blossom in the history of Chinese arts and crafts, but a key cultural heritage of the human kind. The paper introduces the works of bamboo engraving from the features of times, craftsmanship, ordinary shapes and values.

### I. Periods and Artistic Styles of Bamboo Engraving

Seen from documents and relics, the development of bamboo engraving can be roughly divided into the period before the Ming Dynasty, the Ming Dynasty, the early Qing Dynasty, the late Qing Dynasty and the Republic of China with unique features of their times.

#### 1.1　Before the Ming Dynasty

Though bamboo engraving has a long history, it is not very easy to preserve bamboo articles worn by time and natural conditions, so few of them survive nowadays. However, there are some practical bamboo articles unearthed. Some bamboo articles of early periods, e.g. bamboo slips for recording and daily articles were discovered in recent excavations. In 2002, a bamboo strip woven mat was unearthed in Kuahuqiao Remains in Xiaoshan, Zhejiang about 8000 years ago. The ladder-shaped mat, with three broken sides and one complete side slanting to the edge and crisscrossed wooden strips woven into a wider part, was known to be the earliest bamboo product so far in China①. In addition, over 200 bamboo woven articles of the Neolithic Age about 5000 years ago, including mats and baskets, were unearthed in Qianshanyang Remains in Huzhou, Zhejiang, and some very complicated patterns, such as, "plum blossom eyes" and "braid buttons" were created with high skills②.

Lacquer wares were popular during the Warring States, Qin and Han Periods and some of the lacquer wares had bamboo matrixes. Bamboo articles tend to be more artistic under the influence of lacquer art. Three bamboo cups unearthed from the Chu Tombs, the Warring States Period in Jiangling, Hubei were made of cylinder bamboo joints with bamboo caps lacquered in black or red colors③. Two colored bamboo ladles with relief and openwork dragon patterns were unearthed from No. 1 Western Han Tomb of Mawangdui in Changsha, Hunan④. Two bamboo brush pen pipes with "Baima Zuo" and "Shihu Zuo" in intaglio seal characters were unearthed from Wuwei Han Tomb in Gansu⑤. The above-mentioned cultural objects bear sound proof that craftsmen knew how to engrave the bamboo articles before the Warring States Period, which are precious materials to study the history of bamboo engraving.

As recorded in *Book of Southern Qi · Biography of Ming Sengshao* in the Northern and Southern Periods, Emperor Gaodi of State Qi once granted a bamboo ruyi to Ming Sengshao, a famous hermit at that time. And the poem of Yu Xin, a famous writer in the Northern Zhou Period once mentioned wine cups made of bamboo roots, and they are both works of art.

Bamboo engraving became an artistic style during the Tang and Song Dynasties and there are few survivors now. During this period, bamboo articles were delicately made and the engraving art, with different craftsmanship, tend to be complete. The earliest bamboo object existing now is a Shakuhachi, of 43.6cm long, flat engraved with delicate patterns of figures, flowers and birds in the Tang Dynasty collected in Shoso-in, Nara, Japan. As recorded in *Knowledge of Pictures* by Guo Xuruo of the Song Dynasty, Wang Qi, governor of Dezhou, the Tang Dynasty collected a brush pen pipe engraved with the beautiful patterns of figures, pavilions, clouds, rivers and poetic lines, which was the shallow hair engraving. Moreover, cages made by Zan Cheng, a bamboo engraving artist during Reign Gaozong of the Song Dynasty were described vividly as having delicate and fine patterns of palaces, figures, landscape, flowers, trees and birds in openwork on bamboo strips and Zan Cheng was the earliest bamboo artist recorded in history. A remnant of a bamboo figure, of 7cm long and 2.7cm wide, engraved with patterns of courtyard, pines and rockeries on the background of grass and square brocade, was unearthed from Western Xia No. 8 Tomb, Yinchuan, Ningxia⑥ and it was the only bamboo remnant of the Southern Song Dynasty existing at present. Anyway, bamboo engraving did not form an art school of its own since bamboo engraving objects were seldom seen or carried in records, while bamboo engraving was more often than not applied for the decoration of articles.

1.2  The Ming Dynasty

Bamboo engraving became a specialized art after the mid-Ming Dynasty when refined scholars preferred to paint, design and engrave by themselves, and then "it became a specialization since it handed down from father to son, from the master to students, or it was imitated by others in private". During Reign Jiaqing, the bamboo engraving was classified into Jinling School (belonging to Nanjing now) and Jiading School (belonging to Shanghai now) based on different localities and skills, recorded in *Records of Bamboo Engravers* by Jin Yuanyu in Jiading. Jinling School attaches importance to simplicity and use of lines, mainly shallow engraving on fan ribs of elegance and primitive simplicity. Jiading School focuses fine and practical craftsmanship of patterns of landscape, figures, birds, beasts and pavilions, mainly openwork, deep and relief engraving, first on ornaments, later on display objects of pen holders, pen rests, poem tubes and chess boxes.

Zhu He (with the literary name of Ziming, courtesy name of Songlin, active from Reign Jiajing to Reign Wanli), initiator of Jiading School, his son Zhu Ying (with the literary name of Qingfu, courtesy name of

Xiaosong, active during 1520-1587) and his grandson Zhu Zhizheng (with the courtesy name of Sansong, active during 1570-1650) were renowned as "Three Zhu of Jiading". They were proficient in bamboo engraving, developing from fine and delicate craftsmanship, to a balanced artistic style of simplicity with complication, to the perfection of using knives freely as pens. In all, the works of Zhu's family are featured by deep engraving with five or six layers to show the three dimensional effect. Its carving of figures aimed at primitive simplicity, carving of birds and flowers after the refined and delicate atmosphere of Xu Xi, creating a new style of integrating bamboo engraving and painting, and exerting a great influence on the further generations of bamboo and wood engraving.

Pioneer of Jinling School, Pu Zhongqian, with another name of Pu Cheng and literary name of Zhongqian, was born in 1582, 10$^{th}$ year during Reign Wanli in Nanjing. His style was featured by shallow engraving, in particular, on twisting bamboo roots or charred bamboo. He would make an exquisite work of art in an instant by making full use of the natural shape or feature of the material. *Annals of Taiping Prefecture* said, "With his original ideas, he could make delicate rhinoceros horn, jade and bamboo objects in openwork engraving". Besides, he could make bamboo objects of fan ribs, wine cups, pen holders and pen rests as well as rosewood, ebony and ivory objects with high quality, but they were seldom seen. Due to his high reputation, most of the works of art of later generations carrying his inscriptions with complicated and vulgar patterns were fakes.

Apart from Jiading and Jinling Schools, Zhang Xihuang, renowned as "master of flat engraving", was famous at the end of the Ming Dynasty. With his flat and shallow engraving skills, he engraved fine and exquisite patterns of landscape on bamboo products, however, few of them survived. The patterns of landscape usually feature panoramic scenery, pavilions, terraces and buildings in regularity and neatness, and the figures, commonly of only 1cm tall, were dotted in the scenery and their facial expressions were expressed in postures. In addition, the flat engraved poetic lines in running and regular scripts, together with inscriptions, seals and landscape make up a quasi-work of painting and calligraphy.

Openwork, deep and high relief engraving of the Zhu's, shallow engraving and knife chiseling of the Pu's and flat engraving of the Zhang's formed three distinct styles of bamboo engraving in the Ming Dynasty.

1.3 The Early Qing Dynasty

The period from the early Qing Dynasty to Reign Qianlong was the golden period of bamboo engraving, since it witnessed the diversification both in decorative themes and engraving skills. Generally, the artistic style followed the high relief and openwork engraving of the Zhu's in the Ming Dynasty, however some artists, by integrating different engraving skills, created a lot of works with great vitality and colors, e.g. "Seven Worthy Men of the Bamboo Forest", "Chess Game", "Listening to Pines", "Watching Waterfalls", "Red Cliff" reflecting the artistic taste of refined scholars. Besides, there emerged a lot of works with the themes of "Auspiciousness", "Good Luck for Ten Thousand Years", "Eight Immortals' Offering Birthday Celebrations", with simple and novel styles, excellent shapes, exquisite engraving, smooth sides and edges. And there were more varieties, e.g. poem tubes, pen holders, incense holders, arm rests, ink beds, pen washers, figures, immortals and Buddhas, crabs and toads. In addition, prevalent in this period was the revival of many antique objects. Actually, the bamboo engraving art was pushed to the summit with the industrious efforts of many masters, e.g. thin relief engraving of Wu Zhifan, 3-D circular engraving of Brother Feng's, landscape deep engraving of Zhou Hao, shallow engraving of Pan Xifeng.

Wu Zhifan, with the literary name of Luzhen, courtesy name of Donghai Daoren, was born in Jiading, Jiangsu. He, proficient in the engraving of figures, flowers and birds, running and grass scripts, during pre-Kangxi Reign, was highly valued by the scholars at that period and his works were selected as tributes to the Treasury. Apart from 3-D circular engraving, he was more skillful in relief painting of two types. The first type was that, by developing and carrying forward the engraving style of the Zhu's, he adopted high relief engraving with different layers; the bulging part similar to circular engraving, while the low part in openwork engraving. The second was the innovative shallow relief between the Zhu's high relief and shallow relief after Longmen Stone Engraving and "thin relief engraving" became the jargon for Wu's shallow engraving. It was done by outlining the theme in shallow relief engraving on a background of spacious surroundings, and the natural texture of the bamboo was exposed by scraping away the other parts. There even emerged a school headed by Wu Zhifan, called "Thin Relief Engraving" and many of his works still survived now.

The Feng's family in Jiading, the representation of 3-D circular engraving, with successive generations of bamboo engravers, was famous until Reign Xianfeng and Reign Tongzhi, in particular, brothers of Feng Xijue (with the literary name of Jinhou), Feng Xilu (with the literary name of Yihou, courtesy name of Lianchi in his later years), and Feng Xizhang (with the literary name of Hanhou) during Reign Kangxi were most famous. In 1703, 42$^{nd}$ year during Reign Kangxi, Feng Xilu and Feng Xizhang were summoned to work in Hall of Mental Cultivation in the Forbidden City of Beijing, and were famous far and wide, and thus began the service of bamboo engravers in palaces. Brothers of Feng, mainly carrying forward the style of the Zhu's, were proficient in circular engraving of works with novel shapes. With the materials of bamboo roots, they created some figures favored by the folk, e.g. "Liu Hai Teasing the Toad", "Monk Cloth Bag". Unlike the primitive and simple style of the Zhu's, they, with consummate openwork engraving and fine delineation, created the minute parts vividly, such as, the position of hands and feet, texture of clothes, facial expressions, especially, the wrinkled skin and white hair, rib bones, prominent?laryngeals and teeth of the old, however, few of the authentic works survived and many works with their names were fakes.

Zhou Zhiyan, the most famous bamboo engraver from Reign Yongzheng to Reign Qianlong of the Qing Dynasty with another name of Hao, literary name of Jinzhan, courtesy name of Zhiyan, Xueqiao and Yaofeng Shanren, was born in 1685, 24$^{th}$ year during Reign Kangxi in Jiading, Jiangsu (Shanghai) and died in 1717, 38$^{th}$ year during Reign Kangxi. He was proficient in running and grass scripts, bamboo painting and engraving, in particular, of landscape. During Reigns Yongzheng and Qianlong, he, by breaking the tradition of the Northern School in bamboo engraving, pioneered a new school of engraving in following the Southern School. Without a sketch, he engraved with his knife on the bamboo smoothly and the wrinkled method he adopted in engraving the landscape was vivid and lively. In addition, his way of cutting was usually of smooth and fluent intaglio cut, with patterns outlined in wrinkled method. Zhou Zhiyan was a key figure in the mid Qing Dynasty in the changes of styles since he exerted great influence on the future generations by carrying forward the excellent tradition of bamboo engraving in Jiading and brought forward the new style.

Pan Xifeng, another bamboo engraver active during Reign Qianlong wit the literary name of Tonggang, courtesy name of Laotong, was born in Xinchang, Zhejiang and moved to Yangzhou in his later years. He, commended by Zheng Banqiao as the No.1 bamboo engraver after Pu Zhongqian, was considered to be of Jinling School. As he was proficient in shallow engraving, with simple, continuous and forceful lines and strokes, and he would engrave inscriptions and seals with the compositions of famous works. He was particularly skillful in shallow engraving chrysanthemums on arm rests and the objects he engraved were scraped and polished to their perfection.

## 1.4 The Late Qing Dynasty

The period from Reign Jiaqing to Reign Xuantong was characterized by a transition from openwork and circular engraving to shallow and flat engraving both in craftsmanship and design compositions. Bamboo engravers, no longer those men of letters capable of painting and engraving themselves, could only engrave by getting designs from painters and the bamboo engravers, just like engravers of common workshops, only pursued the similarity in the forms instead of the meticulous engraving. Though they were some famous bamboo engravers recorded in the late Qing Dynasty, e.g. Wang Heng (active in Reign Jiaqing and Reign Daoguang with literary names of Meilin, Zhongwen, Maolin, courtesy name of Linshanren) who was good at shallow relief engraving and engraving small regular characters; Fang Jie (1800—1838, with the literary name of Juping, courtesy name of Zhi'an, born in Huangyan) who was good at figure portraits, there are few great masters. At that time, Haishang Painting School, with the themes of past stories, theatrical figures and legends, was popular in the world of painting and bamboo engravers, naturally influenced by this fashion, tried to imitate those of the famous painters and calligraphers and the copied works reminded viewers of the original creators at a glance. The representative figure of the trend was Cai Zhao (with the original name of Zhaochu, literary name of Rongzhuang, born in Xiaoshan and active during Reigns Xianfeng and Tongzhi) who was good at copying. He, usually cooperating with Ren Xiong, an engraver from Xiaoshan, created a lot of block printing and bamboo works and he once engraved 100 sets of bamboo ribs for Wang Ling in Xiaoshan with patterns of landscape, flowers, ladies and Buddhist statues. Painted and engraved by Ren Xiong, the patterns in intaglio vividly reflected his artistic and aesthetic appreciation and were very famous. At the same time, with the popularity of epigraphic studies, calligraphy and inscriptions engraved on bamboo articles were mostly of epigraphic rubbings of inscriptions and forms, which were rather rare in former periods. There were of sand, walnut and orange peel matrixes in terms of craftsmanship and there emerged new styles of pipe tubes, bamboo root wine cups, jars for the game of go, cap cylinders, box of cigarettes, box of stamps and yellow pasting fans in terms of shapes.

## 1.5 The Republic of China

The Republic of China, generally speaking, witnessed the decline of bamboo engraving and different bamboo engraving skills, though there were some bamboo engravers like Shi Dajing, Tan Weide, Wang Jieren, Zhang Zhiyu, Gong Yuzhang, Pan Xingyong, Jin Shaotang, Jin Shaofang and Zhi Ci'an. The bamboo engravers then, neither talented in poems and essays nor good at painting and calligraphy, only did their engraving by imitating the works of others. The artistic creation pioneered by refined painters and calligraphers was gradually changed from the main stream to a branch of the art and to simple styles. The popular bamboo articles were mainly pen holders, arm rests, fan ribs, card boxes, seals, pipe tubes, cigarette holders, glasses boxes and bamboo canes.

## II. Craftsmanship of Bamboo Engraving

The bamboo engraving is roughly classified into circular, intaglio and relief engraving, and subclassified into hair, shallow, deep, shallow relief, high relief, openwork and flat engravings.

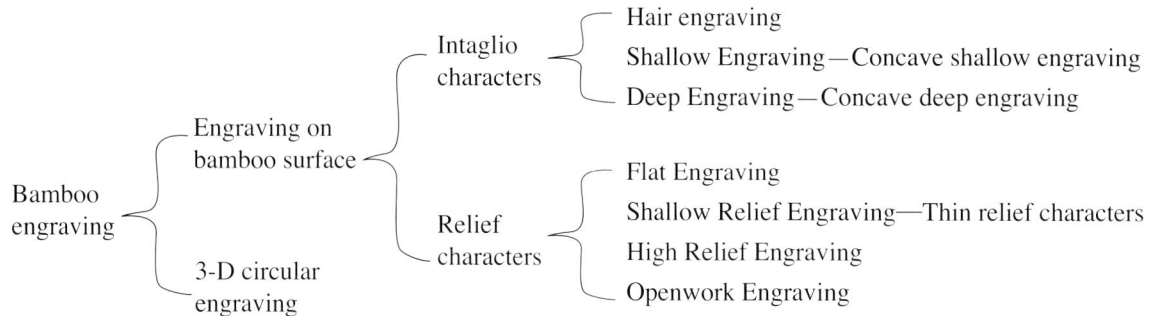

Bamboo engraving
- Engraving on bamboo surface
  - Intaglio characters
    - Hair engraving
    - Shallow Engraving—Concave shallow engraving
    - Deep Engraving—Concave deep engraving
  - Relief characters
    - Flat Engraving
    - Shallow Relief Engraving—Thin relief characters
    - High Relief Engraving
    - Openwork Engraving
- 3-D circular engraving

Bamboo engraving is generally classified into these categories, but usually two or more engravings are applied onto one bamboo work, with one predominant method. Synchronic judgment of the bamboo works mainly depends on the sequence of craftsmanship in history. The major bamboo engravings are introduced as follows.

Concave deep engraving: the patterns are concaved into the plain and smooth surfaces of bamboos and the patterns can be as thick as five or six layers. It started in the pre-Qing Dynasty and was seldom used after Reign Qianlong and Reign Jiaqing.

Flat engraving, also called skin engraving, is done by making use of the differences between bamboo green and bamboo flesh in the texture and color, the former fine, smooth, jade-like and of light color, while the latter with silk lines; and the color of bamboo flesh will be darker with the passage of time. Usually bamboo green engraving patterns are kept and thin green parts are scraped away. The master engravers of bamboo green are skillful at different ways of cutting since the bamboo skin should be kept intact in engraving and different layers of the landscape patterns can be shown by having more or less bamboo skin left. Flat engraving, originated in the Tang Dynasty, was seldom seen in the period after the Tang and it was not until Zhang Xihuang, an engraver in the end of the Ming, was famous for his flat engraving, that it was rediscovered by the artistic world and the current works were all made after the Qing Dynasty.

Thin relief engraving: shallow relief patterns are engraved by scraping away all the bamboo bases or the bases around, and then the minute parts are engraved. It was initiated by Wu Zhifan during Reign Kangxi of the Qing Dynasty.

Bamboo engraved base patterns are classified into smooth base, openwork base, base with geometrical patterns, e.g. patterns of thunders, waves, scalps and brocade, and sand base, belonging to relief engraving, consisting of fine sand, rough sand, walnut and orange peel bases. The sandy based first appeared in Reign Daoguang, the Qing Dynasty.

Bamboo yellow pasting, a unique engraving craftsmanship also called bamboo yellow, is made by scraping the thin bamboo yellow inside the bamboo, and then the yellow is boiled, pressed, pasted onto the wooden matrix (mostly yellow rosewood), and engraved with decorations. The craftsmanship, originated in the early Qing Dynasty in Shaoyang, Hunan, was most prosperous during Reign Qianlong and Reign Jiaqing and widely used in palaces. Subsequently, the products were made in Jiading of Jiangsu, Huangyan of Zhejiang, Jiang'an of Sichuan and

Shanghang of Fujian.

III. Common Bamboo Objects

Strictly speaking, it is classified into bamboo root and bamboo cane engraving.

3.1 Bamboo root engraving

Bamboo roots with more knots are suitable for making root engraving since they are of primitive simplicity. Usually, craftsmen make use of the natural shapes of bamboo roots to make objects of ornament, and the common objects feature immortals, figures, flying birds and beasts, miniature landscape, flowers, fruits and vegetables, object imitations, brush pen washers and pen rests. The rhinoceros horn-shaped bamboo root cups and bamboo root seals are most famous.

The period from the end of the Ming to the early Qing Dynasty witnessed the popularity of rhinoceros horn-shaped bamboo root cups and therefore, bamboo root cups in shapes of rhinoceros horns were prevalent in the early Qing Dynasty and the patterns mainly feature pines with cranes, deer, squirrels, figures, plum blossoms and bamboo leaves. In addition, the men of letters of the early Qing favored rhinoceros horn-shaped bamboo root cups with patterns of lofty themes, however, this kind of cups were no longer made after Reign Kangxi.

Bamboo root seals, initiated in the Qing Dynasty, were based on the natural shapes of the roots, with seal characters engraved on flat bottoms.

3.2 Bamboo cane engraving

Bamboo canes can be made into round brush pen holders and incense holders with round joints, or into arm rests and fan ribs with bamboo sections or strips.

Common objects:

Pen holders: the display objects in the study engraved with patterns of paintings and calligraphy came out in large numbers in the late Ming Dynasty. After Reign Wanli, the pen holders became larger and thicker, engraving changing from plain one to shallow relief, to high relief, to openwork, and finally to circular effects. This kind of openwork pen holders was characteristic of the bamboo engraving in the late Ming while "thin relief characters" were popular in the early Qing Dynasty. In the mid-Qing Dynasty, the pen holders, with diameters up to 20cm, carried deep engraved patterns and in the late Qing, they became smaller with shallow relief or intaglio engraving. Besides, in Reign Guangxu and Reign Qianlong, pen holders with flat engraving were popular.

Incense holders, also called fragrance holders, were openwork bamboo tubes with wooden covers popular from the Ming to mid-Qing dynasty. In the Ming, they usually featured patterns of dragons, while in the Qing, they featured patterns of folk stories and after Reign Yongzheng, the engraving on the holders was of complicated and delicate layers and those made in Reign Qianlong were most beautiful. However, in the late Qing Dynasty, incense holders were seldom seen since they were probably replaced by incense burners.

Arm rests, used by men of letters in writing to avoid getting stained in hands, were of the shapes of "tiles" with patterns of calligraphy and paintings on the front. Since they were not only used as stationery, but full of artistic taste, they had long been favored by refined scholars. There were few bamboo arm rests of the Ming Dynasty, usually without patterns, at present. And the arm rests of the Qing usually did not carry patterns on the backs and the arm rests with patterns on the backs appeared at the transition from the Qing Dynasty to the early Republic of China.

Paper weights, in the shapes of rulers, were also called "paper rulers". They featured patterns of orchids, bamboo and twin dragons and usually had smooth bottoms.

Boxes, used for holding books, notes, ink sticks, seals and ink stones, were usually square and round with covers. They were decorated with different openwork patterns or inlaid with jewels or shells, and with delicate paintings or calligraphy on the covers.

Fan ribs were usually made in flat engraving, and with different patterns on the surface.

Display objects: bamboo display objects of the Ming Dynasty were usually immortal and Buddhist statues. In the Qing Dynasty, there were more varieties, e.g. Buddhist hands, ruyi, mountains, lotuses and crabs, toads, animals and fruits. The figures and animals in the Ming and early Qing had rhinoceros horn or rosewood eyes, and in the late Qing Dynasty, bead eyes. In particular, the display objects during Reign Qianlong, e.g. wine cups, washers, wine containers, jars, tripods, goblets and bottles, were in imitation of the ancient bronze objects of the Xia, Shang and Zhou Dynasties both in shapes and patterns, and they were exquisite, beautiful and full of artistic value.

Apart from the above objects, there were poem tubes, letter tubes, flower receptacles, cages, pen washers, pen pipes, snuff bottles and incense pendants, etc.

IV. Appraisal of Bamboo Works of Art

Exquisite bamboo objects, of high artistic significance and historical and economic values as well, are much favored by the people. Commonly speaking, there are several criteria.

First, engraving craftsmanship. The value of engraving lies in craftsmanship rather than minute work, in elegance rather than vulgarity. A good bamboo work, within a limited space, is created with the magic engraving of different layers, of harmonious combinations of dense and thin cuts, therefore, a superb one should be created with the innovative ideas of the engravers both in painting, calligraphy and engraving.

Second, inscriptions. Commonly speaking, those art works with inscriptions, in particular, with inscriptions of celebrities are better, though there are some works with high artistic value, but without inscriptions. There are four fake methods: copy carving, fake carving, inscription added and fabrication and sometimes, it is rather difficult to tell those works with perfect engraving craftsmanship, but with fake inscriptions.

Third, period. The works with longer history carry high values since it is not very easy to preserve the bamboo objects. Moreover, the colors can be various: light yellow, brownish yellow, brownish red, dark red and deep brown and the objects with longer history are usually of dark colors, and those objects as red as cherries, or like the colors of ambers are the gems and those black ones are inferior. The objects of the Qing Dynasty were usually of grayish brown and those of the Ming were of dark red.

Fourth, quality. It includes the shapes, sizes and conditions of objects.

To sum up, values of the objects are determined upon the comprehensive appraisal since the above items are interrelated.

Chai Xuanhua

Notes:

(1) Zhejiang Cultural Relics Archeological Research Institute, Xiaoshan Museum: *Kuahuqiao—One of the Archeological Reports of Puyang River Basin*, Cultural Relics Press, 2004

(2) Zhejiang Cultural Relics Administration Committee: "Reports of the First and Second Excavations in Qianshanyang Remains", Wuxing, *Acta Archaeologica Sinica*, No. 2, 1960

(3) Hubei Provincial Museum, Jingzhou District Museum, Jiangling County Cultural Relics Working Team: "Briefing of Excavation of Paimashan Chu Tombs in Jiangling, Hubei", *Archeology*, No. 3, 1973

(4) *No.1 Han Tomb of Mawangdui*, Changsha, Cultural Relics Press, 1973

(5) Gansu Provincial Museum, Wuwei County Cultural Center: "Briefing of Excavation of Three Han Tombs in Mozuizi, Wuwei", *Archeology*, No.12, 1972

(6) Ningxia Hui Autonomous Region Museum: "Briefing of Excavation of Western Xia No.8 Tomb", *Archeology*, No.8, 1978

Bibliography:

(1) Wang Shixiang: *Bamboo Engraving*, People's Fine Arts Publishing House, June 1992

(2) Ye Yi, Tan Zhicheng: *Chinese Bamboo Engraving Art*, Hong Kong Museum of Art, 1982

(3) Li Jun: *Bamboo Engraving in the Ming and Qing Dynasties*, Ningbo Publishing House, 2005

(4) He Chongzheng, Cheng Zhaoping, Cai Guoshen: *Bamboo, Wood and Ivory Engraving*, Shanghai Culture Publishing House, April 2002

(5) *Treasures of Engraving—Best Selections of Bamboo Engraving in the Ming and Qing Dynasties*, National Museum of History, Taibei, September 2005

# 目　录 Contents

图 版
PICTURES

## 竹根雕刘海戏金蟾坐像　明

连座高19厘米

BAMBOO ROOT ENGRAVING: SEATED STATUE OF "LIU HAI TEASING GOLDEN TOAD", THE MING DYNASTY

Height with Seat: 19 cm

竹根由于竹肉较多，比较适合做圆雕作品，故人物像、山子等摆件大多由竹根雕刻。

坐像为竹根圆雕，宽衣左袒，宽嘴大鼻，眼珠以犀角镶嵌，整个开脸具有明代朱氏一派的风格。左手撑于左腿上，右手捧蟾，铜钱却吊在右腰上，与常见的刘海戏金蟾略有不同。像座为黄杨木雕刻，作波涛状，与坐像互为呼应。

Bamboo roots, due to thickness, are great for circular engraving, in particular, for the ornaments of figure statues and miniature landscape.

This seated statue, a circular bamboo root engraving, features loose clothes, wide mouth, big nose and rhinoceros-horn-inlaid eyeballs, which coincides with the Zhu's style of the Ming Dynasty. Liu Hai, with the left hand on the left leg, the right hand holding the toad and copper coins hanging on the right waist, is different from the commonly seen Liu Hai. The seat, engraved out of Chinese box twig, corresponds to the seating statue with its wave patterns.

### 竹根雕高士坐像　明

高9厘米、底径5厘米

BAMBOO ROOT ENGRAVING: SEATED STATUE OF A SENIOR MONK, THE MING DYNASTY

Height: 9 cm, Bottom Diameter: 5 cm

坐像肥头大耳，眉眼、嘴鼻宽厚，具有明代塑像的开脸特征。竹根几无竹青，没有深红发亮的皮壳，但棱角之处已被盘摩得圆润光滑。此类坐像在明代比较少见。

The statue features a large head, big ears, wide and thick eyes, mouth and nose, which coincides with the facial characteristics of the Ming Dynasty statues. The root, without bamboo green or dark red bamboo shell, has round and smooth edges. This kind of statues is rare in the Ming Dynasty.

## 竹根雕刘海戏金蟾像　明

高13.5厘米

BAMBOO ROOT ENGRAVING: STATUE OF "LIU HAI TEASING GOLDEN TOAD", THE MING DYNASTY

Height: 13.5 cm

圆雕刘海戏金蟾与众不同，刘海骑于金蟾之上，金蟾显得比较硕大，但蟾首被刘海左手按住，右手掂着铜钱，双眼俯视金蟾，大鼻咧嘴，呈现出玩金蟾于掌股之间的神态。虽然面相有小损，但明晚期的风格也是显而易见的。

This unique circular engravure features Liu Hai's dominance in teasing by riding on a big toad, the left hand pressing the toad head, the right hand holding the copper cash, eyes glaring at the toad. Besides, Liu Hai has a big nose and is grinning. Though the face is damaged, its style of the late Ming Dynasty is distinctive.

**竹根雕刘海戏金蟾坐像**　明末清初
高15厘米
BAMBOO ROOT ENGRAVING: SEATED STATUE OF "LIU HAI TEASING GOLDEN TOAD", AT THE TURN OF THE MING
AND QING DYNASTIES
Height: 15cm

坐像以竹根圆雕而成，刘海憨态可掬，秃顶披发，大鼻咧嘴，耳垂丰腴，其睛以犀角点之，脸相从不同的角度看都各呈意趣。一手抚脚，一手持钱戏金蟾，虽是坐姿，却动感十足。作品当初是髹朱漆的，因岁月久远，坐像上留下了斑驳的痕迹。

Circular engraved out of a bamboo root, the seated statue features a charmingly playful Liu Hai with a bald head top, loose hair, a big nose and a grinning face, fat earlobes and rhinoceros-horn-inlaid eyeballs. In addition, Liu Hai is holding his foot with one hand, teasing the toad with the other. Though seated, it is dynamic. Seen from different perspectives, the face shows different atmospheres. It is originally a red lacquered product, and the lacquer wears away due to the passage of times.

## 竹根雕刘海戏金蟾坐像　清

高22厘米

BAMBOO ROOT ENGRAVING: SEATED STATUE OF "LIU HAI TEASING GOLDEN TOAD" , THE QING DYNASTY

Height: 22 cm

坐像包浆红润，为竹根圆雕作品。刘海憨笑可掬，坐于洞石假山之上，双手持一串古钱，欲戏弄匍匐于脚下之金蟾。从开脸和洞石工艺看，似为清早期作品。

Circular engraved out of a bamboo root, the seated statue, with ruddy wrapping, features a charmingly playful Liu Hai sitting on the rockery with hands holding a string of coins and teasing the golden toad on his feet. It is an early-Qing product seen from its face and crafts of holes caves and mountains.

**竹根雕达摩立像**　清

高12.8厘米

BAMBOO ROOT ENGRAVING: STANDING STATUE OF DHARMA, THE QING DYNASTY

Height: 12.8 cm

立像以竹根圆雕而成，高额虬须，肥耳大鼻，衣袖宽大，气定神闲，视一苇渡海若闲庭信步。竹根雕虽没有红润的皮色，但包浆润洁，乃盘摩日久之功。

Circular engraved out of a bamboo root, the statue features a calm and sedated Dharma with a high forehead, thick moustaches, fat ears, a big nose and loose clothes. Though the bamboo root engraving does not have ruddy skin color, its lustrous wrapping shows the touch of times.

## 竹雕佛手纹杯　明

高9、最大径10厘米

BAMBOO ROOT ENGRAVING: CUP WITH A PATTERN OF A BUDDHA HAND, THE MING DYNASTY

Height: 9 cm, Maximal Diameter: 10 cm

竹雕取材于竹根处，深刻、镂雕折枝佛手纹，枝叶盘绕于杯身，叶片肥厚，舒张转侧，果实饱满，错落于枝叶中。竹雕杯盘摩日久，皮色深红，全无斧琢之痕，颇有古风。

Engraved out of a bamboo root, the cup has the pattern of an openwork Buddha hand and twining branches and leaves around the cup. In addition, there are fruits among the big and thick leaves. The bamboo cup, with the passage of times, shows a crimson skin color and an ancient flavor.

## 竹根雕古松纹杯　清

高8.2、最大径10.7厘米

BAMBOO ROOT ENGRAVING: CUP WITH PINE PATTERNS, THE QING DYNASTY

Height: 8.2 cm, Maximal Diameter: 10.7 cm

杯子以竹根圆雕成古松形，浮雕、镂雕松针、鳞皮、枝干，并以盘曲的枝干为把，松针硕大细密，刻工粗细相谐，洒脱流畅，乃竹雕中之精品。

This cup is circular engraved out of a bamboo root with openwork and relief pine needles, barks and trunks. The handle is a twining trunk and pine needles are big and delicate. With meticulous and smooth engraving, it is a gem of bamboo engraving.

**竹根雕松树纹杯**　清

高12、最大径10.2厘米

BAMBOO ROOT ENGRAVING: CUP WITH PINE PATTERNS, THE QING DYNASTY

Height: 12cm, Maximal Diameter: 10.2 cm

杯子为竹根圆雕作品，古松形，以打洼、凸节表现枝干苍劲古拙，松针疏朗错落，颇有韵致。杯子成器后，髹以朱漆，较一般竹杯光亮。原配红木底座。

This cup is circular engraved out of a bamboo root with an old pine pattern. The old and strong trunks and well-arranged pine needles show a unique flavor. The cup, painted in red lacquer, is brighter than the other bamboo cups. It was originally fitted with a mahogany base.

## 竹根雕鹿衔灵芝杯　清

高5.6厘米

BAMBOO ROOT ENGRAVING: CUP WITH A PATTERN OF A DEER HOLDING A LUCID GANODERMA, THE
QING DYNASTY

Height: 5.6 cm

杯以竹根为之，浑身布满竹纹之星点，如梨皮一般。鹿造型写实，口衔灵芝，寓意长寿。竹雕正放如摆件，倒过来鹿首面部和鹿角构成一个平面，成为杯足，鹿腹为杯身，真乃匠心独运。
曾见有杯身内嵌入依形而制银杯的竹根雕鹿衔灵芝杯，故该类竹雕是带有实用功能的艺术品。

This cup, engraved out of a bamboo root, is like the pear peel with bamboo dots around. The pattern of a deer holding a lucid ganoderma in the mouth means longevity. It is uniquely shaped since it is an ornament when placed upwards and it is transformed to a cup upside down, with the face of the deer and antlers forming a surface as the foot of the cup and the belly of the deer as the cup.

In addition, there are cups with the pattern of a deer holding a lucid ganoderma embedded into a silver cup and this kind of bamboo engraving is a work of art with practical functions.

## 竹根雕方斗杯　清

两耳间宽6.7厘米

BAMBOO ROOT ENGRAVING: SQUARE-FILTER-SHAPED CUP, THE QING DYNASTY

Width between Two Ears: 6.7cm

杯子为竹根镂雕而成，呈方斗状，左右各置一个简易夔龙耳，前面刻"酌以"，后面刻"大升"，字上填以青绿色。方斗杯小器大样，刻"酌以大升"隐喻饮者之海量，乃小中见大之雅具。

The cup, openwork engraved out of a bamboo root, has two simple dragon-shaped ears. Four characters of "Zhuo Yi" and "Da Sheng" are carved in the front and the back respectively in turquoise color. Four characters combined mean the drinkers' great capacity for wine.

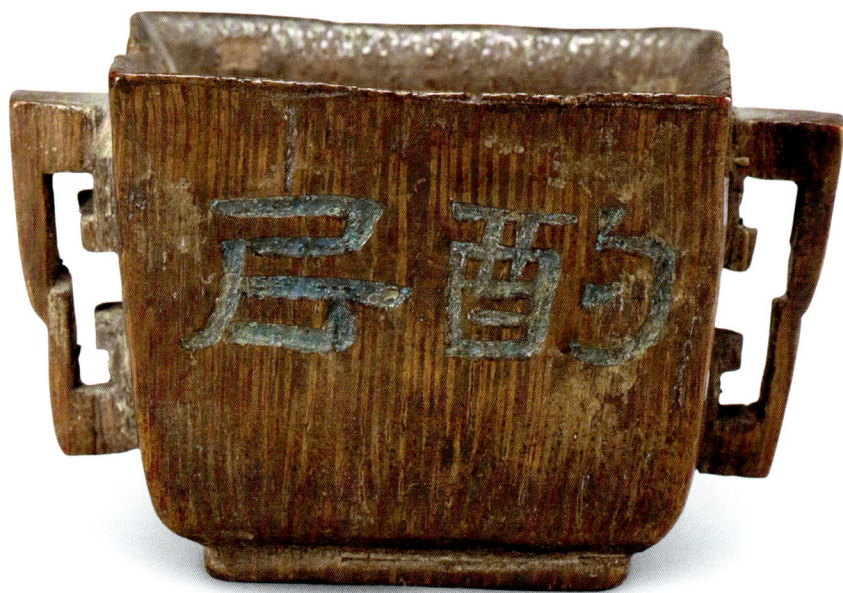

## 竹刻松荫高士雅集图笔筒　明

高14.8、直径11.4厘米

BAMBOO BRUSH POT ENGRAVED WITH PATTERNS OF PINES AND LITERATI, THE MING DYNASTY

Height: 14.8 cm, Diameter: 11.4 cm

因年代久远，笔筒已呈暗红色，但仍可看出明嘉定一派浮雕加镂雕的技法。小小笔筒以通景方式展现听琴、论诗、造访三个场景。十个人物，姿态各异，通过细腻的刀法，展现了弹琴者的怡然忘我，听琴者侧身前倾，专注琴韵；茶童不亦乐乎地忙碌；论诗者或站或立，或执笔论书，或执卷聆听；造访者欣然捋须与书童略显羞涩的神情互为映衬。方寸之间定格了四五百年前那场即将开始的文人雅集。笔筒以竹茎为之，是竹刻作品中最常见的形制，也是竹刻艺术品中最具文人气息的。

The brush pot, though turning dark red with the passage of times, still retains the relief engraving and openwork of the Jiading School of the Ming Dynasty. It features three scenes of listening to the music of Qin, discussing poems and paying visits. Ten figures of different postures, with meticulous engraving, show a lively picture: the detachment of the Qin player and the preoccupation of Qin music listeners, the busy tea boy, the standing or seated literati discussing poems or listening to poem discussions and the delightful visitor and the timid study companion.

The brush pot, out of a bamboo cane, is a common variety of bamboo products with strong atmosphere of literati.

## 竹刻山水花草纹笔筒　明

高12.5、直径10.5厘米

BAMBOO BRUSH POT ENGRAVED WITH PATTERNS OF LANDSCAPE AND FLOWERS, THE MING DYNASTY

Height: 12.5 cm, Diameter: 10.5 cm

笔筒呈深红色，山水和花草不成比例，反映了竹刻匠人对造化的理解。花草的叶和蕊阴阳转侧，非常生动。纹饰的棱角已非常光润，非岁月久远不能为。

The dark red brush pot, with disproportionate landscape and flower patterns, reflects the craftsmen's understanding of nature. The leaves and buds, with great fluency of engraving, are lively and vivid. The edges of the patterns, with the passage of times, have become smooth.

竹刻山水花草纹笔筒　明

高12.5、直径10.5厘米

BAMBOO BRUSH POT ENGRAVED WITH PATTERNS OF LANDSCAPE AND FLOWERS, THE MING DYNASTY

### 竹刻松荫纹枰图笔筒　明

高14、直径9.1厘米

BAMBOO BRUSH POT ENGRAVED WITH PATTERNS OF PINES AND SENIORS PLAYING CHESS, THE MING DYNASTY

Height: 14 cm, Diameter: 9.1 cm

笔筒面上呈深红色，深雕、镂雕深山松荫下三位老者正纹枰对弈。刻者只重意境，甚至大面积镂空竹面，来表现深度和立体感，体现了高超的驾驭空间的本领。

The dark red brush pot, with deep engraving and openwork, features three seniors playing chess. The craftsman, by paying attention to the whole atmosphere, depth and three-dimensional effect with the large openwork on the surface, shows the superb mastery of the space.

竹刻松荫纹枰图笔筒　明

高14、直径9.1厘米

BAMBOO BRUSH POT ENGRAVED WITH PATTERNS OF PINES AND SENIORS PLAYING CHESS, THE MING DYNASTY

Height: 14 cm, Diameter: 9.1 cm

## 竹刻松荫赏古图笔筒　清

高15、直径11.5厘米

BAMBOO BRUSH POT ENGRAVED WITH A PATTERN OF FOUR SENIORS APPRECIATING PAINTINGS UNDER A PINE TREE, THE QING DYNASTY

Height: 15 cm, Diameter: 11.5 cm

竹刻高浮雕松荫赏古图，以刀为笔，刻画了正在赏画的四位老人的不同形态。末尾落款"沙神芝刻"。

沙神芝，字笠甫，浙江嘉兴人。工篆、隶，学怀素狂草，笔力雄健。擅画梅花，兼善篆刻。能于笔筒内刻书、画。

The brush pot, with relief engraving, features different postures of four seniors appreciating a painting. And there is an inscription of "Engraved by Sha Shenzhi".

Sha Shenzhi, with the literary name of Lifu, was born in Jiaxing, Zhejiang in the Qing Dynasty. He was proficient in seal and official scripts and also learned the wild running script from Huaisu. In addition, he was good at painting plum blossoms and engraving, in particular, engraving calligraphy and paintings inside the brush pots.

## 竹刻锦灰堆笔筒　清

高13.8、直径6.8厘米

BAMBOO BRUSH POT ENGRAVED WITH FRAGMENTED PATTERNS, THE QING DYNASTY

Height: 13.8 cm, Diameter: 6.8 cm

笔筒棕红色包浆，纹饰为平阳布、五铢钱、汉瓦当、晋文砖等古物叠加的锦灰堆，左侧楷书题"古泉，汉瓦，晋砖文"。落款"欣如摹，元生刻"。

元生，即吴廷康（1799~？），字元生，号康甫，又号赞甫，一作赞府，别号晋斋，晚号茹芝，安徽桐城人。官浙中数十年。与何绍基至交。精金石考据，篆、隶铁笔，直窥汉人。亦工刻竹。有砖癖，辑慕陶轩古砖录。余事写梅、兰，寥寥数笔，金石之气盎然。年近九十卒，身后遗墨，始为人所重。

欣如亦是当时竹刻名家。

The brush pot, with brownish red wrapping, features fragmented patterns of Pingyang cloth, five-zhu coins, tiles of the Han Dynasty and bricks of the Jin Dynasty. On the left are the regular characters of "Guquan, tiles of the Han and brick inscriptions of the Jin" and the inscriptions of "Imitated by Xinru and engraved by Yuansheng".

Wu Tingkang (1799-?), with the literary name of Yuansheng, courtesy names of Kangfu, Zanfu, Jinzhai and Ruzhi, was born in Tongcheng, Anhui. He was an official for over 10 years and was a good friend to He Shaoji. Besides, he was proficient in epigraphic studies, interpretation of ancient texts, official scripts and seal characters, bamboo engraving and in writing about plum blossoms and orchids. Living to an old age of 90, he left behind a lot of precious calligraphy works and was honored by later generations.

Xinru was another famous bamboo engraver at that time.

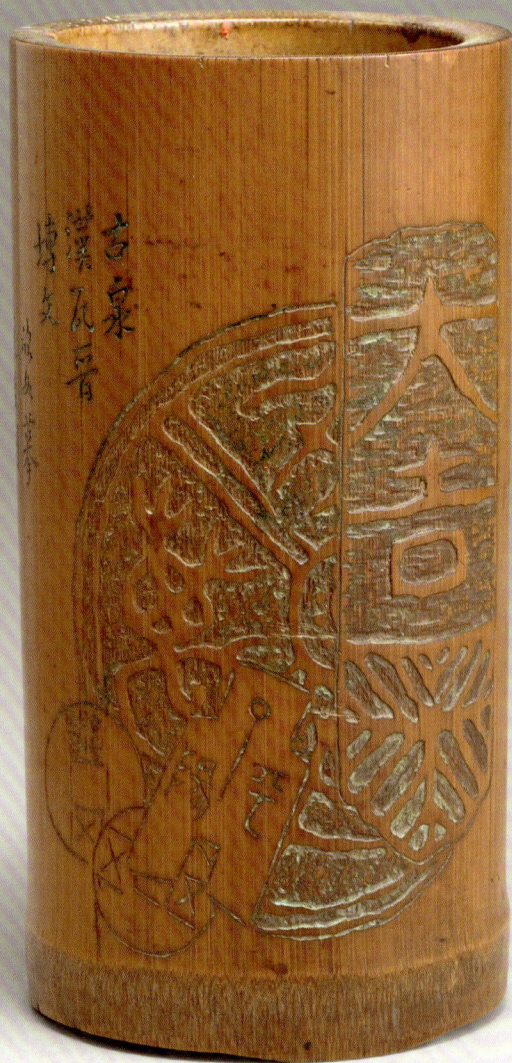

### 竹雕竹节诗文笔筒　清

高13.5、直径7厘米

BAMBOO BRUSH POT ENGRAVED WITH PATTERNS OF BAMBOO JOINTS, POEMS AND ESSAYS, THE QING DYNASTY

Height: 13.5 cm, Diameter: 7 cm

笔筒以竹为之，再刻上竹节纹，包浆红润，上首题"戊子仲秋日"，下刻五言诗一首："皮相原无节，知君蕴酿深。凌霄气方盛，转眼绿成阴"。落款"云谷居士题"。诗文下方从左到右依次横排为圆章"尤如水至止"，横题"九如文"，方章"如松柏之茂"。

云谷，即林泉，字云谷，清代福建晋江人。书、画无不考究。善四声，工篆、隶，小楷得钟、王法。

The brush pot, with patterns of bamboo joints and ruddy wrapping, features a poem depicting lush greenery in autumn, several inscriptions of "Autumn day in year Wuzi", "Inscribed by Yungu Lay Buddhist", the seals of "Like water to its stopping", "Like essays" and "Like the luxuriant pines and cypresses".

Lin Quan, with the literary name of Yungu, was born in Jinjiang, Fujian in the Qing Dynasty. He was proficient in painting, calligraphy and official scripts, seal characters and regular scripts.

皮　知　凌　轉
相　君　霄　眼
原　蘊　氣　綠
衆　釀　方　陰
鄙　遲　盛　陲

戊子仲秋林書

丁亥秋日題

文和九

## 竹雕白菜纹笔筒　　清

高12.5、直径6厘米

BAMBOO BRUSH POT ENGRAVED WITH A PATTERNS OF CHINESE CABBAGE, THE QING DYNASTY

Height: 12.5 cm, Diameter: 6 cm

笔筒包浆红润，于小草地中刻一大白菜。纹饰后面题"樵白阳山人本于碧云红树伴吟楼，少谷"。

少谷，即韩小山，字少谷，清代江苏扬州人。《竹人录》记载的名家之一，精于刻竹，兼通书法，字迹娟秀不失古雅。

The brush pot, with ruddy wrapping, features a big Chinese cabbage on the grassland and the inscriptions of "Mobaiyang Shanren, clear clouds, red trees with the pavilion, Shaogu".

Han Xiaoshan, with the literary name of Shaogu, was born in Yangzhou, Jiangsu in the Qing Dynasty. One of the famous bamboo engravers in *Records of bamboo Engravers*, he was proficient in bamboo engraving and calligraphy.

## 竹雕髹漆刻诗文笔筒　清

高12.5、直径7.3厘米

LACQUERED BAMBOO BRUSH POT ENGRAVED WITH PATTERNS OF POEMS AND ESSAYS, THE QING DYNASTY

Height: 12.5 cm, Diameter: 7.3 cm

笔筒以竹茎为胎骨，髹以朱漆，漆上以楷书、草书各刻七言诗一首。楷书七言诗："玉净花明理鬓余，轻描翠黛竟舒徐。有图尚拟联同志，直欲方之太史书。"草书七言诗："高卷湘帘出艳妆，不关花气自闻香。蝶蜂也似缠头客，乱逐游踪上下狂。"落款"古吴孙仁山制于三十六鸳鸯馆"。

三十六鸳鸯馆位于苏州拙政园内，孙仁山应是苏州一带的竹刻家。

The brush pot, with the bamboo cane as the matrix, is lacquered with red paint and inscribed with two seven-character poems describing the beautiful landscape in regular and running scripts. In addition, there are inscriptions of "Made by Sun Renshan in Pavilion of Thirty-six Mandarin Ducks of Suzhou".

Pavilion of Thirty-six Mandarin Ducks is located in the Garden of Humble Administration of Suzhou and Sun Renshen might be the bamboo engraver in Suzhou.

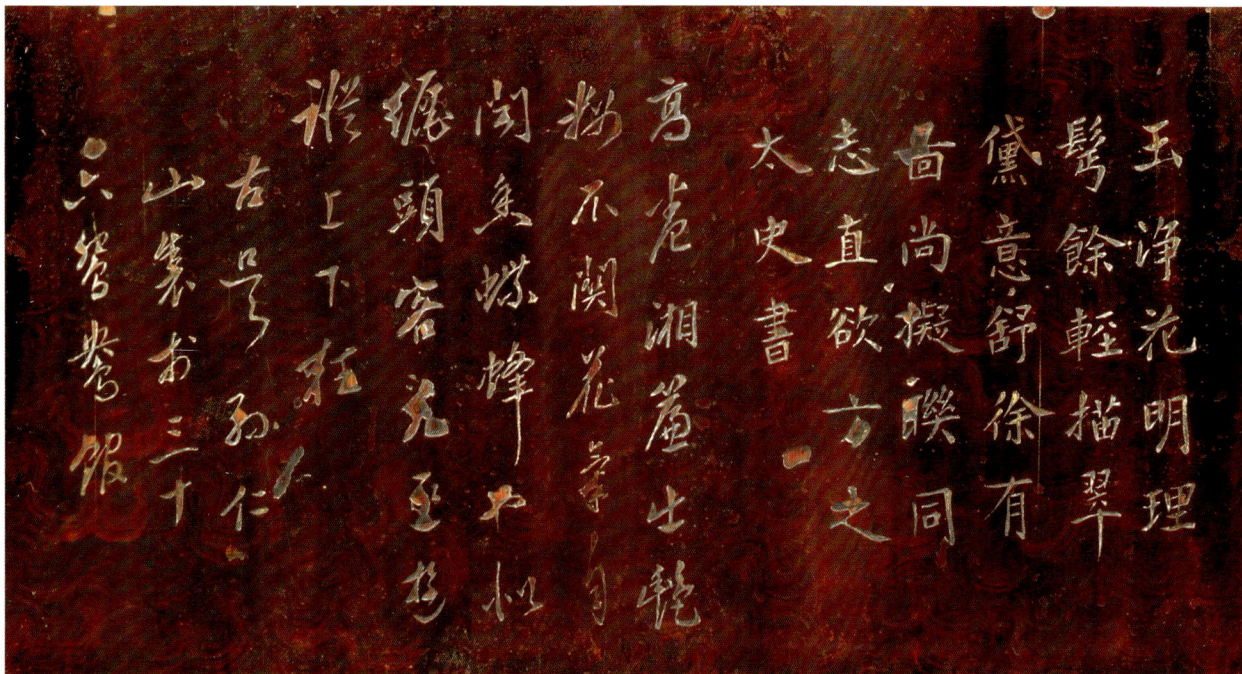

竹雕髹漆刻诗文笔筒　清

朱文公一日喫茶畢徐謂第子曰物之甘者喫過
必酸苦者喫過却甘茶是苦物喫過却甘問
此理如何曰也是一箇道理如始作憂勤終
於逸樂

竹汀居士錢大昕書

## 竹雕指日高升纹臂搁　　清

高23.5、宽7.5厘米

BAMBOO ARM REST ENGRAVED WITH A PATTERN OF PROMOTION AS THE SUN RISES, THE QING DYNASTY

Height: 23.5cm, Width: 7.5cm

臂搁浮雕边框，框内浮雕山水纹背景，一老人举手指向天空的太阳，寓意"指日高升"，为中国古代艺术的传统题材。此种纹饰刻于臂搁之上，更有对学子的激励作用。

The arm rest, with a relief engraving frame, features a traditional theme in ancient Chinese art: an old man raising his hand towards the sun in the sky signifying "promotion" in the background of landscape patterns in relief engraving. The pattern on the arm rest is also used for encouraging the students to work harder.

## 竹刻咏竹诗臂搁　　清

长22.5厘米

BAMBOO ARM REST ENGRAVED WITH A POEM EULOGIZING BAMBOOS, THE QING DYNASTY

Length: 22.5 cm

臂搁做工考究，皮色棕黄，章草刻咏竹诗曰："惟尔劲节，惟尔虚心。舍之则藏，用之则行。"落款"云樵"，章"徐氏"。

云樵，即徐枢，字宗岐，号云樵，清代嘉定隐士。周颢弟子。画得师传，以刻竹为游戏，俱微妙可思。又善琢砚，得周颢遗法。

This delicate arm rest, with brownish yellow skin color, features a poem eulogizing the loftiness of bamboos. In addition, there are inscriptions of "Yunqiao" and a seal of "Xu Shi".

Xu Shu, with the literary name of Zongqi and courtesy name of Yunqiao and hermit of Jiading, was the disciple of Zhou Hao in the Qing Dynasty. He was proficient in bamboo and ink slab engraving.

惟尔劲節恒尔虚心舍之

勿藏用之勿行

雪樵 [印]

## 竹雕留青诗文臂搁　　清

高24、宽6.5厘米

FLAT CARVED BAMBOO ARM REST WITH A SEVEN-CHARACTER POEM, THE QING DYNASTY

Height: 24 cm, Width: 6.5 cm

臂搁留青刻草书七言诗句"笔阵独扫千人军"，落款"弘业"。草书字虽不多，布局大小有致，颇具章法。

The arm rest features a seven-character poem in grass scripts, "Power of pen surpasses an army of one thousand soldiers" and inscriptions of "Hongye". The characters are neatly and orderly organized.

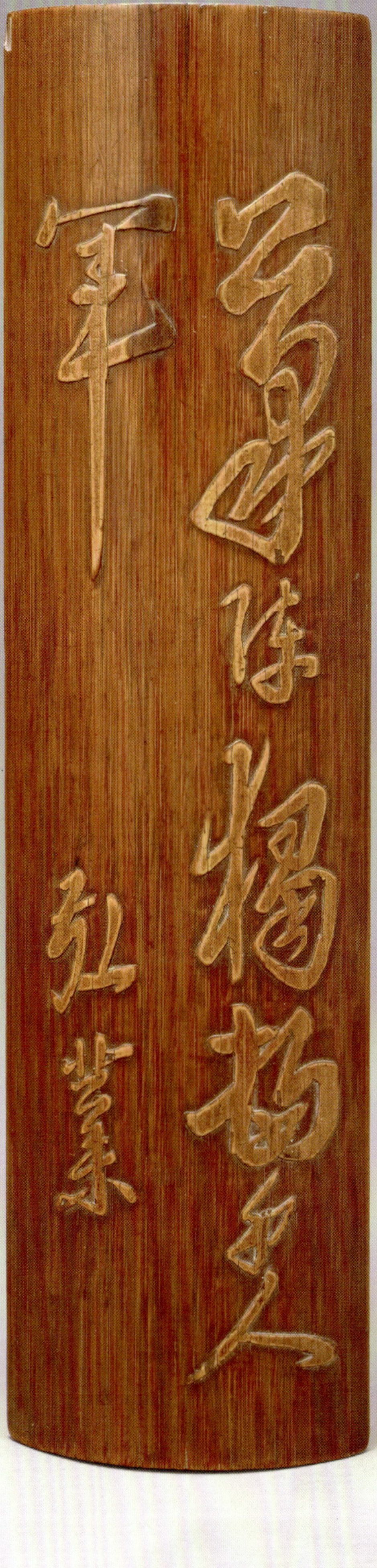

## 浅刻山水纹臂搁　清

高23.5、宽8厘米

BAMBOO ARM REST ENGRAVED WITH A PATTERN OF LANDSCAPE IN SHALLOW ENGRAVING, THE QING DYNASTY

Height: 23.5 cm, Width: 8 cm

臂搁皮色深红润洁，画面浅刻山水纹，寒山枯木闲亭，以刀为笔，正侧自如，应景而变，山体应势皴擦，虽是芝岩一路，功力并不见逊。上部题范成大《横塘》诗句：“年年送客横塘路，细雨垂杨系画船。”落款“即仙”。

即仙，即陆遵书，字即仙，一字芙苑，一作扶远，号得岑，嘉定人。清乾隆三十三年举人。遵书工山水及梅竹松石，杂卉蔬果。山水本娄东法，烟云深秀，丘壑不穷可与张鹏翀抗行。乾隆四十八年尝作寒林夕照图等。

The arm rest, with dark red lustrous skin color, features the pattern of landscape: solitary mountains, withered trees and a pavilion in shallow engraving. The mountains are engraved with wrinkled methods. Besides, there is a poem of "Heng Tang" by Fan Chengda and the inscriptions of "Jixian".

Lu Zunshu, with the literary names of Jixian, Fuyuan and courtesy name of Decen, was born in Jiading and was the successful candidate in the provincial-level imperial examination in 33[th] year during Reign Qianlong of the Qing Dynasty. He was proficient in painting landscape, plum blossoms, pines, mountains, flowers and fruits, and in particular, his landscape painting, with charming mists and clouds, can be comparable to that of Zhang Pengchong. He created Forest at Sunset in 48th year during Reign Qianlong.

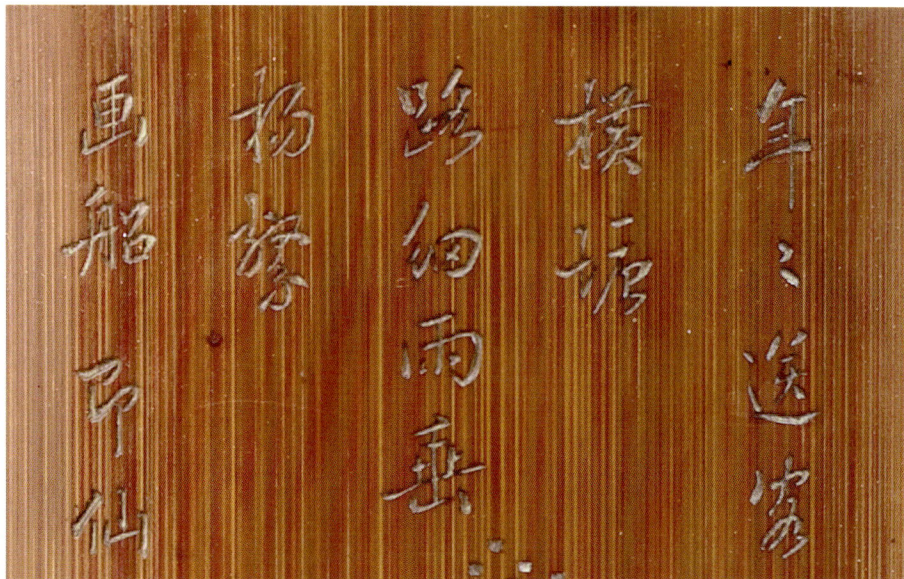

## 竹刻梅花诗文臂搁　清

长27厘米

BAMBOO ARM REST ENGRAVED WITH PATTERNS OF PLUM BLOSSOMS AND A POEM, THE QING DYNASTY

Length: 27cm

臂搁皮色棕黄，浅刻折枝梅花，疏密有致，左上部题诗曰："添得平泉诗入妙，一枝鹤顶配风流。"落款"子函"。子函，即温葆深，字子函，号明叔，江苏上元（今南京）人，善翰墨，清道光二年壬午恩科三甲三名进士，选庶吉士，官至宗人府丞、左副都御使、户部礼部侍郎。著有《春树斋丛说》。臂搁似为自刻自用作品。

The arm rest, with brownish yellow skin color, features several branches of plum blossoms in shallow engraving and a poem describing the beautiful landscape with the inscriptions of "Zihan".

Wen Baoshen, with the literary name of Zihan and courtesy name of Mingshu, was born in Shangyuan, Jiangsu (Nanjing at present) and good at calligraphy. He, one of the three successful candidates in the highest imperial examination in 2nd year during Reign Daoguang, assumed many high posts in his lifetime. The arm rest seems to be a product engraved and used by himself.

添得平泉詩入妙一枝
鶴頂記風流　子安

**竹刻诗文臂搁**　　清
高23.5、宽7.5厘米
BAMBOO ARM REST ENGRAVED WITH POETIC LINES, THE QING DYNASTY
Height: 23.5 cm, Width: 7.5 cm

臂搁背部红木托底，做工考究。正面满刻诗文，字体俊秀，行楷阴文刻："昔人谓洛神赋象凌波神，赵松雪所得之陈集贤者十三行，仅二百五十字，系晋麻纸，字画神逸，墨彩飞动，为天下法书冠。癸丑小春月上浣书"。落款"筠谷山人"。
筠谷山人，即清代嘉定竹刻名家杨谦。

This delicate arm rest, with a mahogany base at the back, features a poem in intaglio running script and elegant characters describing the superb calligraphy works of Chen Jixian collected by Zhao Songxue, though with 250 words in 13 lines and the inscriptions of "Jungu Shanren".

Jungu Shanren refers to Yang Qian, a famous bamboo engraver in Jiading, the Qing Dynasty.

昔人善論神賦象瓌波神趙松雪所得之
陳集吳者十三行僅二百五十字繫晉麻箋
字盡神逸玉躰死動為天下法以冠
癸丑小春月上浣書

筠石山人

## 竹刻古梅纹臂搁　　清

高29.5、宽7厘米

**BAMBOO ARM REST ENGRAVED WITH A PATTERN OF PLUM BLOSSOMS, THE QING DYNASTY**

Height: 29.5 cm, Width: 7 cm

臂搁右边偏下刻倒垂昂首古梅一枝，左上阴刻行楷书诗句："斜靠一枝清入梦，低垂半树冷无香。"落款"道光辛卯秋，次闲写并题"。下押方章"赵"字。左下另有一行铭款"问源嘱，莲淑偶作"。辛卯为道光十一年（1831年）。赵次闲（1781～1860年），字次闲，号献父、穆生、宝月山人，浙江杭州人。工书画篆刻，山水师黄子久、倪云林，萧疏幽淡，花卉竹石有明人气息。喜写佛像，为各地居士、丛林所宝。为"西泠八家"之一，近代六十名家之一。
莲淑，即赵丙，字日修，号莲淑，清代江苏甘泉（今扬州）人，工书法，有晋、唐人风范。自以为不工而善书者往往称之。

The arm rest features the pattern of a plum blossom raising its head in the lower right; in the upper left is engraved with a poem in intaglio regular script describing the lofty loneliness of plum blossoms by Zhao Cixian in the autumn of 1831, 11th year during Reign Daoguang at the age of 50 and a square seal of "Zhao". Besides, in the lower left are the inscriptions of "Created by Lianxu".

Zhao Cixian (1781-1860), with the literary name of Cixian and courtesy names of Xianfu, Musheng and Baoyue Shanren, was born in Hangzhou, Zhejiang. He, a student to Huang Zijiu and Ni Yunlin, masters of landscape painting, was proficient in landscape painting and seal engraving. His paintings of flowers, bamboos and mountains, elegant and scattered, are after the style of the painters in the Ming Dynasty. Besides, he was fond of painting Buddhist statues and his paintings were favored by lay Buddhists. He was also renowned as one of the "Eight Masters of Xiling" and "Sixty Masters in the Modern Times".

Zhao Bing, with the literary name of Rixiu and courtesy name of Lianxu, was born in Ganquan, Jiangsu (Yangzhou at present) in the Qing Dynasty. He was proficient in calligraphy and his style was similar to that of the Jin and Tang calligraphers.

**竹刻折枝梅花纹臂搁**　清

高24、宽5.8厘米

BAMBOO ARM REST ENGRAVED WITH A PATTERN OF PLUCKED PLUM BLOSSOMS, THE QING DYNASTY

Height: 24 cm, Width: 5.8 cm

臂搁居中刻折枝梅二枝，左边刻行楷书"癸卯四月次闲墨戏"。癸卯为道光二十三年（1843年），赵次闲62岁。

The arm rest features two plucked plum blossoms in the center and inscriptions of "Written by Cixian in April, year Kuimao" in regular script on the left. Year Kuimao refers to 1843, 23ʳᵈ year during Reign Daoguang when Zhao Cixian was 62 years old.

## 竹刻论书文臂搁　清

高23.5、宽6厘米

BAMBOO ARM REST ENGRAVED WITH AN ESSAY, THE QING DYNASTY

Height: 23.5 cm, Width: 6 cm

臂搁行书阴文刻："大书悬臂，小则不能。臂濡于墨，而渍于纸，何以异于夏月之蝇。不悬而悬惟汝劲。"落款"谨万属录青藤道人铭。次闲"

The arm rest features an essay in intaglio running script commenting on the skills of calligraphers and the inscriptions of "Cixian".

大書縣屑以則不餘縣濡於墨而漬
於紙何以興於夏因之瓶不縣而縣性
汝勁　徐鳥氏辭青藏道人銘製識

## 竹刻前赤壁赋臂搁　清

长23.8厘米

### BAMBOO ARM REST ENGRAVED WITH *FORMER ODE TO THE RED CLIFF*, THE QING DYNASTY

Length: 23.8 cm

臂搁皮色深红，行书阴线刻苏东坡《前赤壁赋》首段一节，书法隽秀流畅。落款"岂甲寅花朝书，墨庄居士"。
墨庄居士，即乔林，字翰园，号西墅，晚号墨庄，清代江苏如皋人。山水不拘家法。工吟咏，善篆隶，得秦汉遗
意，至镌刻晶、玉、瓷、牙、铜、铁、石图章，各臻奇妙。而手制竹根章，尤精雅绝俗。

The arm rest, with dark red skin color, features a section of the first paragraph of *Former Ode to the Red Cliff*
written by Su Dongpo in smooth and elegant intaglio running script. There are inscriptions of "Written by Mozhuang
Lay Buddhist".

Mozhuang Lay Buddhist was the pen name for Qiao Lin. Qiao Lin, with the literary name of Hanyuan and courtesy
names of Xishu and Mozhuang, was born in Rugao, Jiangsu. He was quite unconfined in his calligraphy, and
was proficient in composing poems and calligraphy of seal and official scripts. The crystal, jade, porcelain, ivory,
copper, iron and stone seals engraved by him were all superior articles and the bamboo root seals handmade by
him were consummate.

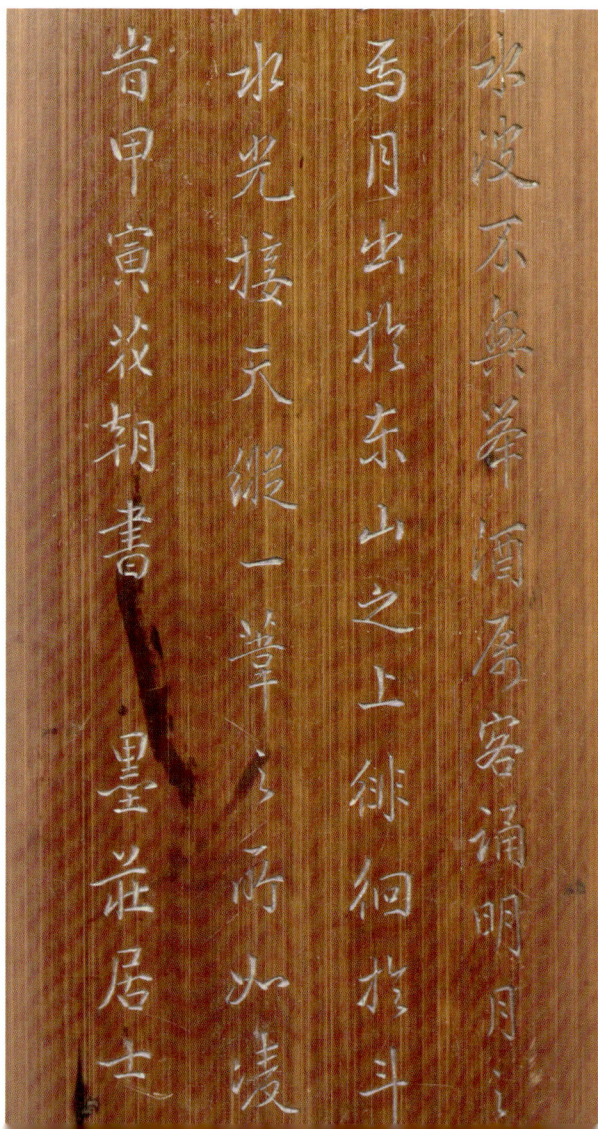

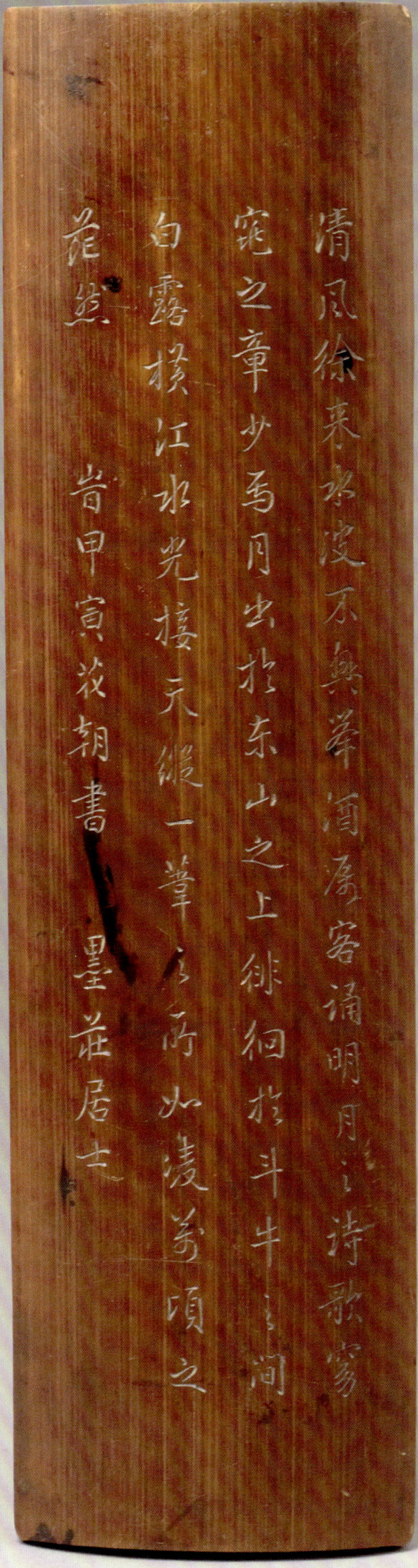

清風徐來水波不興舉酒屬客誦明月之詩歌窈

窕之章少焉月出於東山之上徘徊於斗牛之間

白露橫江水光接天縱一葦之所如凌萬頃之

茫然

甲寅花朝書　墨莊居士

### 竹刻观泉图臂搁　清

高24、宽7厘米
BAMBOO ARM REST ENGRAVED WITH A PATTERN OF WATCHING THE SPRING, THE QING DYNASTY
Height: 24 cm, Width: 7 cm

臂搁阴线深刻写意观泉图，然观泉而不见泉，见人不见脸，画面中部大块空白，留下无限的想象空间。以写意笔法阴线深刻纹饰，一扫晚清简笔浅刻积习。落款"观泉图，盟树生写"。

盟树生，即黄宗起，嘉定人，字韩钦，自号盟树生，晚号止庵。清同治十二年（1873年）举人。工诗及古文辞，精医理，兼善书画篆刻，山水尤在大痴、石谷之间，《清代画史增编》有传。

The arm rest, featuring a free picture of watching the spring in intaglio deep engraving, leaves the viewers the space for imagination with blank space in the center. There are inscriptions of "A picture of watching spring created by Mengshusheng".

Huang Zongqi, with the literary name of Han Qin and courtesy names of Mengshusheng and Zhi'an, was born in Jiading. He was the successful candidate in the provincial-level imperial examination in 1873, 12th year during Reign Tongzhi. In addition, he was proficient in composing poems, studying ancient texts, medicine, painting and calligraphy and engraving.

觀泉圖 聑𥯤叔生寫

## 竹刻诗文臂搁　清

长27厘米

BAMBOO ARM REST ENGRAVED WITH POETIC LINES, THE QING DYNASTY

Length: 27 cm

臂搁皮色深红，书法俊美，行楷书刻"虚以接物，竹本虚心是我师"，落款"光绪丁丑首夏，小亭先生世大人清玩，桐孙刻赠"。丁丑为光绪三年（1877年）。

桐孙，即张惟楙，字韵蕉，号半农，亦号桐孙，别字硕觐，仁和（今杭州）诸生。少而好古，壮而笃学。诗、画、刻印类其人品，娟秀朴茂，天趣盎然。曾手摹汉印数百钮，精拓成谱。是一位治印兼竹刻的文人。

小亭，即蒯增，字小亭，江苏吴江人，活跃于清同治、光绪年间，性极脱略，刻竹治石皆得天趣，善镌刻金石文字，作品多见笔筒与扇骨。

The arm rest, with dark red skin color and beautiful landscape, is engraved with "Treating people modestly and bamboos have modest hearts" in running and regular script, with the inscriptions of "Engraved and donated by Tongsun to Mr. Xiaoting in 1877, 3$^{rd}$ year during Reign Guangxu".

Tongsun, also named Zhang Weimao, has the literary names of Yunjiao, Shuofeng and Student of Renhe as well as courtesy names of Bannong and Tongsun. He was devoted to the ancient studies while young and to the studies of poems, calligraphy and seal engraving in his middle ages, and the poems, calligraphy and seal engraving were a reflection of his decent and simple personality. In addition, he was a man of learning in seal and bamboo engraving and he once compiled his over 100 seal copies into a book.

Kuai Zeng, with the literary name of Xiaoting, was born in Wujiang, Jiangsu and was active during Reign Tongzhi and Reign Guangxu. With his free and easy characters, he followed the natural style in seal and bamboo engraving and his works are mainly shown in pen holders and fan ribs.

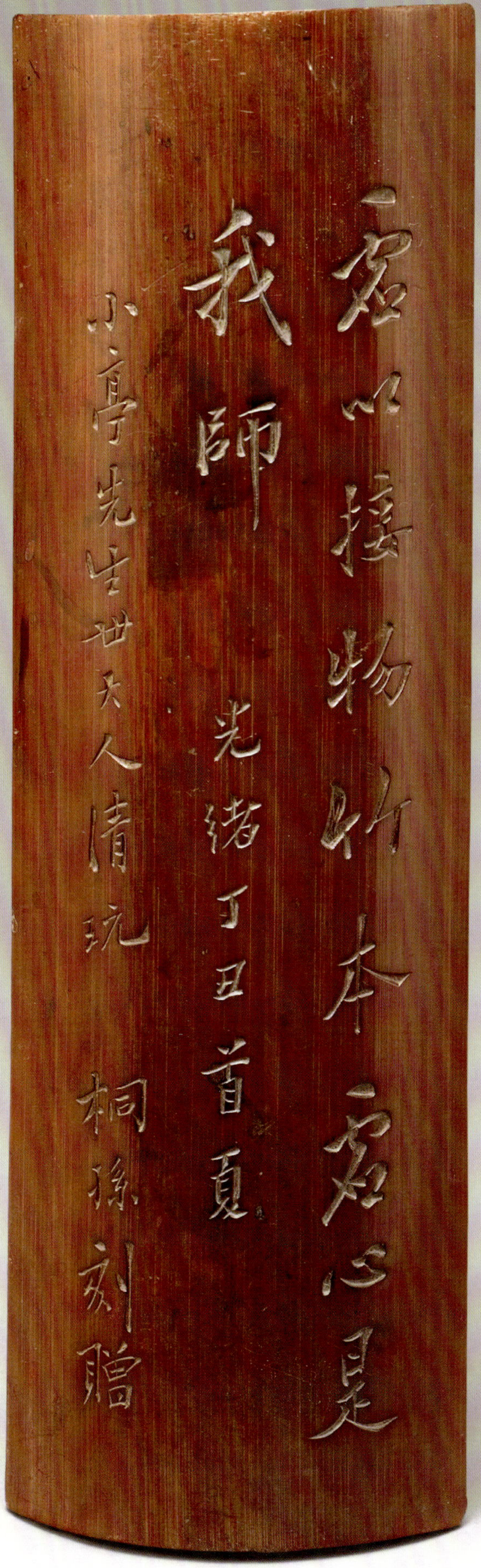

密以接物竹本虛心是
我師

小亭先生世衣人情玩
桐孫劉贈

光緒丁丑首夏

## 竹刻李商隐诗文臂搁　清

高26.5、宽6.5厘米

BAMBOO ARM REST ENGRAVED WITH POETIC LINES OF LI SHANGYIN, THE QING DYNASTY

Height: 26.5 cm, Width: 6.5 cm

臂搁行书阴文刻李商隐《谢河东公和诗启》文句："思将玳瑁，为逸少装；吾愿把珊瑚，与徐陵架笔。"落款"仲华观察大人清玩。鲁琪光"。

鲁琪光（1828~？），字芝友，号戢珊，江西南丰人。鲁垂绅子。同治七年进士，官至济南知府。光绪元年顺天乡试同考官。工书法，书法以欧阳询之乃秀，兼米芾之姿致。乞书者积纸盈屋，有名一时。

The arm rest is engraved with the poetic lines of Li Shangyin, a famous poet in the late Tang Dynasty, in intaglio running script and the inscriptions of "Donated and made by Lu Qiguang to Mr. Zhonghua".

Lu Qiguang (1828~?), with the literary name of Zhiyou and courtesy name of Fushan, was born in Nanfeng, Jiangxi. He was the successful candidate in the imperial examination in 7th year during Reign Tongzhi, and later became magistrate of Jinan Prefecture and the examiner in Shuntian local imperial examination in 1st year during Reign Guangxu. He was proficient in calligraphy, in particular, in following the beauty of Ouyang Xun's and the elegance of Mi Fu's styles. He was famous for a long period.

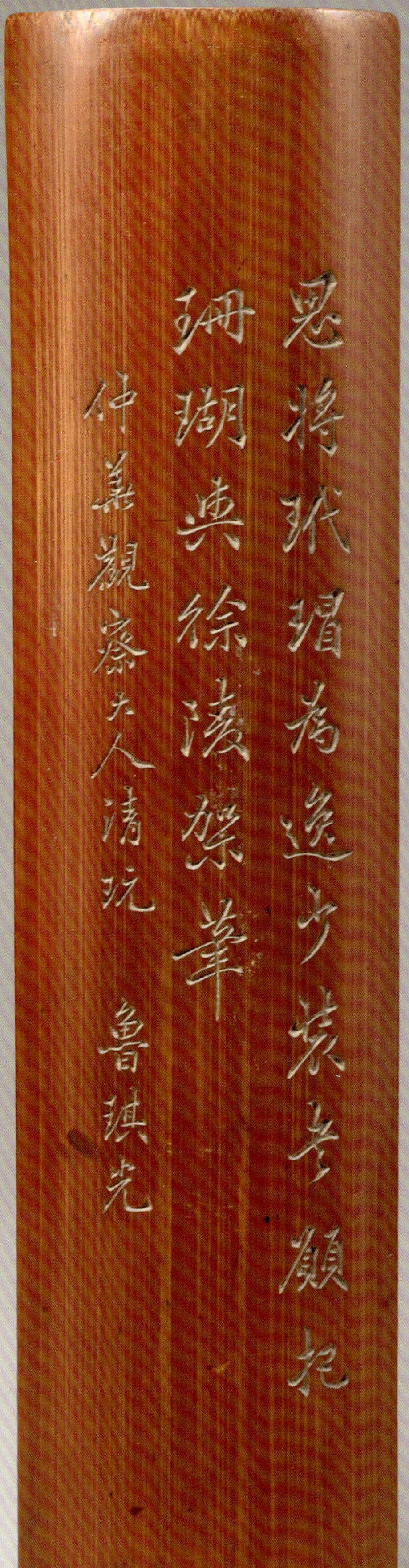

恐將玞瑁為遙岁崖岑顧把

珊瑚與徐陵鎮筆

仲蕪觀察夫人清玩　魯琪光

**竹雕松鹤纹臂搁**　清

长17.8厘米

BAMBOO ARM REST ENGRAVED WITH PATTERNS OF PINES AND CRANES, THE QING DYNASTY

Length: 17.8 cm

臂搁皮色深红，阴线刻松鹤纹，寓意松鹤延年。臂搁上端刻篆书"松"、"鹤"，画右题"乙巳仲夏，庁咺写"。

The arm rest, with dark red skin color, features the patterns of pines and cranes in intaglio lines, signifying longevity. Besides, there are inscriptions of "Song" (pines) and "He" (cranes) in seal character in the upper and the inscriptions of "Written by Qinxuan in summer, year Yisi".

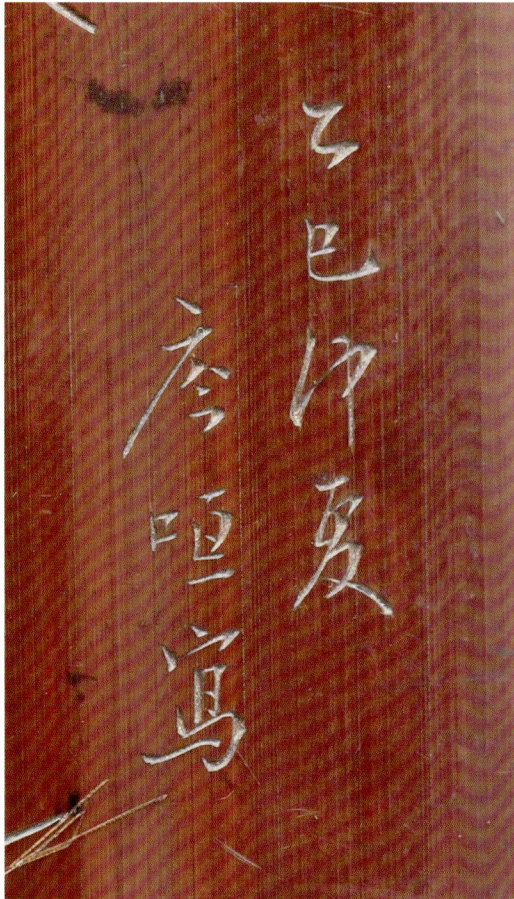

竹雕松鹤纹臂搁　清

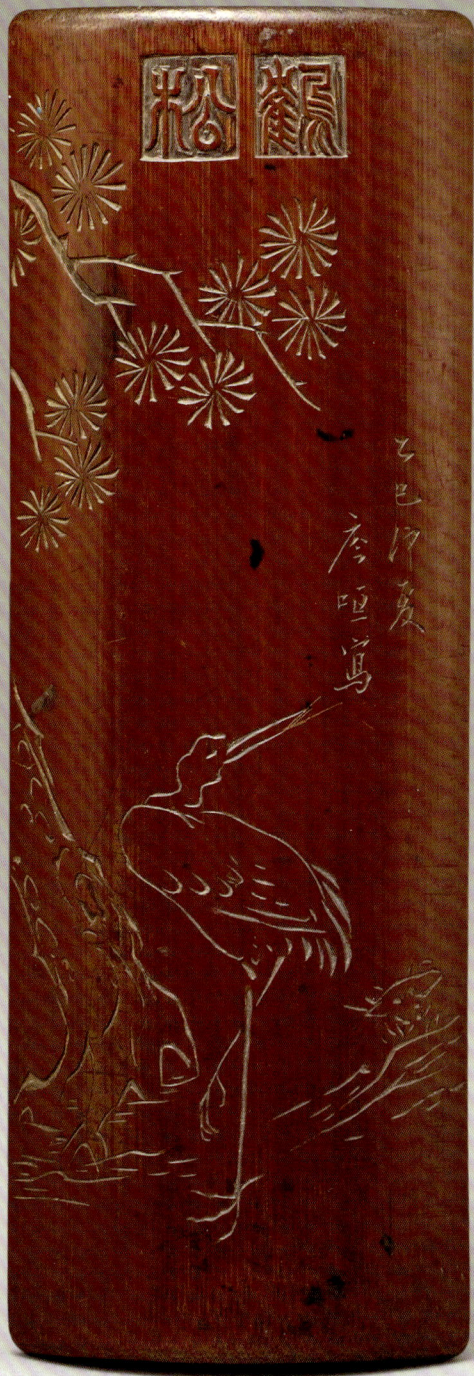

## 竹刻山水纹臂搁　清

长23.2厘米

BAMBOO ARM REST ENGRAVED WITH A PATTERN OF LANDSCAPE, THE QING DYNASTY

Length: 23.2 cm

臂搁皮色深红，阴线刻山水草亭纹，右上题"老木闲亭平细，竹泉山人"。

竹泉山人，即邱钦，字竹泉，清代浙江湖州人。精刻碑文砚铭，尤善鉴别拓本真赝。刻印宗汉，久客云间，以鬻艺自给。清后期以降，竹刻已经成为与治印性质相近的文人雅好的一个组成部分，印人往往兼竹人。清代以"竹泉"为字号的虽然不少，唯有邱钦刻碑治印，鬻艺自给，最有可能是竹刻的作者。

The arm rest, with dark red skin color, features the landscape patterns in intaglio lines and the inscriptions of "Lao Mu Xian Ting Ping Xi and Zhuquan Shanren".

Qiu Qin, with the literary name of Zhuquan, was born in Huzhou, Zhejiang in the Qing Dynasty. He was proficient in engraving tablets, ink stones and in discriminating the authenticity and falsity of rubbings. As recorded in the *Biographies of Seal Engravers*, since the Qing Dynasty, bamboo engraving has been a pastime for seal engravers, and in the Qing Dynasty, though there were many engravers bearing the literary name or the courtesy name of "Zhuquan", Qiu Qin, with his great talent, should be the bamboo engraver.

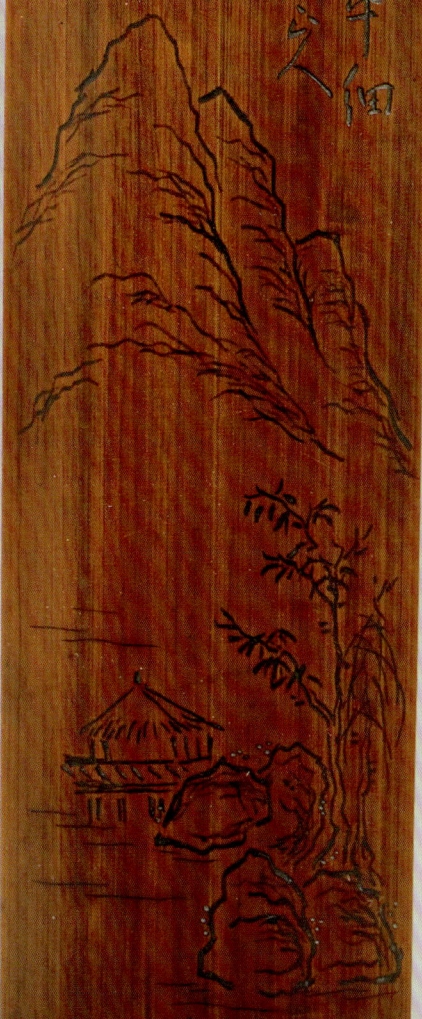

## 竹刻诗文臂搁　清

长27.4厘米

BAMBOO ARM REST ENGRAVED WITH POETIC LINES, THE QING DYNASTY

Length: 27.4 cm

臂搁包浆红润，行书刻七言诗一首："放鹤归来月满天，黄庭扫雪和云眠。夜深不厌风霜冷，谓尔相思已一年。"落款"癸亥重九书，友松"。

友松，即郭福衡，娄县（今上海松江）人，清同治十二年（1872年）举人。性僻诞，多才艺，通六法，尤工画人物，笔致古茂。后往来沪、松，卖画自给。尝于桃核上以烟签刻人物、鸟兽，精妙非常。

The arm rest, with ruddy wrapping, is engraved with a seven-character poem featuring the landscape in winter and the inscriptions of "Engraved by Yousong in year Kuihai".

Yousong, referring to Guo Fuheng, was born in Louxian (Songjiang, Shanghai at present) and was the successful candidate in the provincial-level imperial examination in 1872, 12th year during Reign Tongzhi. As a queer and versatile person, he was quite proficient in figure paintings with an ancient style. Later, he supported himself by selling paintings in Shanghai. In addition, he was adroit in engraving figures, birds and beasts on peach nuts with bamboo sticks.

放鶴歸來月滿天只庵攜雪和雲
眠於溪不厭風霜冷謂尔相思已
一年

癸亥重九書

友松

## 竹刻漱石诗文臂搁　清

长22.8厘米

BAMBOO ARM REST ENGRAVED WITH POETIC LINES BY SHUSHI, THE QING DYNASTY

Length: 22.8 cm

臂搁皮色红润，减地浮雕刻七言诗句："自能洗研拂书几，时亦折花寻酒杯。"阴文方章"漱石"、"西谷"。

漱石，即孙铧，字棣英，号漱石，又号怡堂，清代江苏六合人。尝得宣和印谱原本，简练揣摩，技遂大进。有漱石印存，皆竹根印也。为人伟岸有奇气，负经济才，工书，善琴，韵语绝佳，弈品第一。

西谷，即江尊（1818～1908年），字尊生，号西谷，清代钱塘人，工篆刻，为赵之琛入室弟子。浙中能刻印者多，唯尊传之琛衣钵。

The arm rest, with ruddy wrapping, is engraved with a seven-character poem in relief and two square seals of "Shushi" and "Xigu" in intaglio.

Shushi, referring to Sun Wei with the literary name of Diying and courtesy name of Yitang, was born in Liuhe, Jiangsu. He gained his art of bamboo engraving by copying the *Anthology of Xuanhe Seals*. As a man of integrity, he was devoted to calligraphy, playing Qin instruments and composing poems.

Xigu, referring to Jiangzun (1818-1908) with the literary name of Zunsheng, was born in Qiantang. Proficient in seal engraving, he was the disciple to Zhao Zhichen and was the only one in central Zhejiang to carry forward the legacy of Zhao Zhicheng.

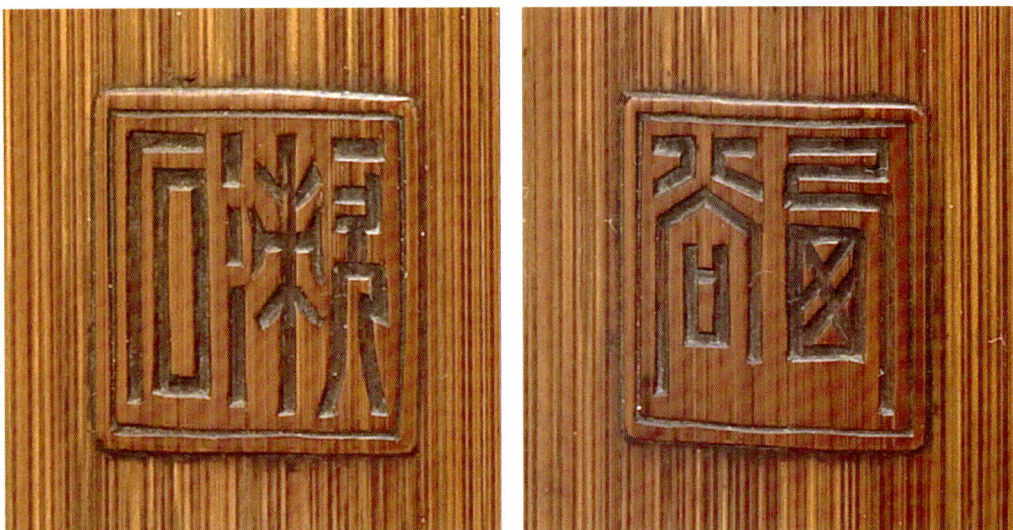

自臨洗研拂光時栽松

氣蜀溫林

## 竹刻西谷诗文臂搁　清

长22厘米

BAMBOO ARM REST ENGRAVED WITH POETIC LINES BY XIGU, THE QING DYNASTY

Length: 22 cm

臂搁行书刻"花落家童未扫，鸟啼山客独眠"。仍然使用减地浮雕技法，落款"漱石"、"西谷"。

The arm rest features the poetic lines of Xigu "Flowers falling, servants do not clean; Birds singing, mountain guests sleep alone" in running script and inscriptions of "Shushi" and "Xigu" in shallow engraving.

竹刻西谷诗文臂搁　清

BAMBOO ARM REST ENGRAVED WITH POETIC LINES BY XIGU, THE QING DYNASTY

玄宗舊事童童赤掃器

啼山青猿吹

## 竹刻蕉荫赏秋图臂搁　清

高28、宽7.5厘米

BAMBOO ARM REST ENGRAVED WITH A PATTERN OF APPRECIATING AUTUMN UNDER THE BANANA TREE, THE QING DYNASTY

Height: 28 cm, Width: 7.5 cm

臂搁以细阴线刻画芭蕉树荫下一书童正侍候一老者饮酒赏景，从左边题字"丙子秋九月"可知是在欣赏秋景。落款"友仁作"。

友仁，即来友仁，清晚期浙江籍竹刻家。

The arm rest features a study companion attending to a senior drinking and appreciating the scenery under the banana tree, with the inscriptions of "September, autumn in year Bingzi" and "Engraved by Youren".

Lai Youren was a bamboo engraver of Zhejiang in the late Qing Dynasty.

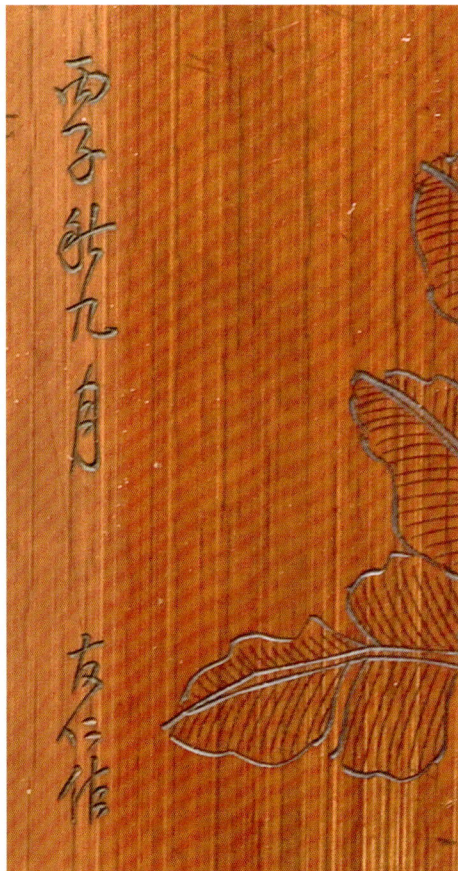

竹刻蕉荫赏秋图臂搁　清

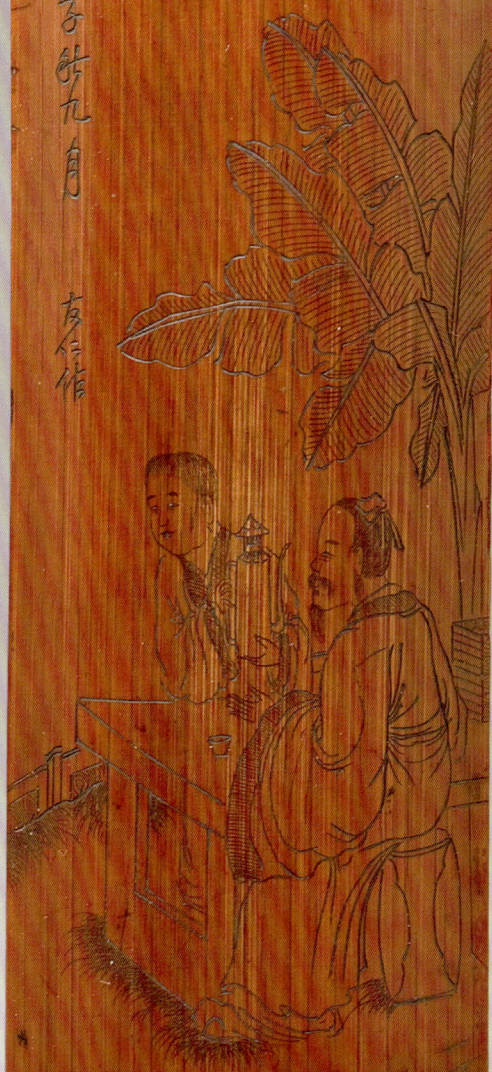

## 竹刻山水纹臂搁　清

高27.5、宽6厘米

BAMBOO ARM REST ENGRAVED WITH A PATTERN OF LANDSCAPE, THE QING DYNASTY

Height: 27.5 cm, Width: 6 cm

臂搁以细阴线刻画山水纹，右上角以较宽阴线刻"水清草茂，风韵箫爽"，落款"寄庵"，章"舟行"。

寄庵，即张应昌（1790～1874年），字仲甫，号寄庵，祖籍钱塘（今杭州），生于归安（今湖州）。清嘉庆十五年（1810年）举人，任内阁中书。道光初年，曾参与编修《仁宗实录》。不久，因病辞职返乡，闭门不出，专以著作，致力于《春秋》之学。兼工诗词，常和杭州词人张景祁相唱酬答。

The arm rest is engraved with the landscape pattern in fine intaglio lines, poetic lines of "Limpid water, luxuriant grass, melodious wind and clear flute song" in wide intaglio lines in the upper right corner, inscriptions of "Ji'an" and the seal of "Zhouxing".

Zhang Yingchang (1790-1874), with the literary name of Zhongfu and courtesy name of Ji'an, was born in Gui'an (Huzhou at present), while his ancestral home was in Qiantang (Hangzhou at present). He was the successful candidate in the provincial-level imperial examination in 1810, 15th year during Reign Jiaqing, the Qing Dynasty. In the first year of Reign Daoguang, he partook in the compilation of *Records of Renzong*. Later, he resigned from office due to bad health and was devoted to writing books in his home, in particular, to the studies of *Spring and Autumn*. Besides, he was proficient in writing poems and comparable to Zhang Jinqi, a famous poet in Hangzhou.

水清草茂
風韻蕭爽
丙戌秋日
竹广圖

## 竹刻朱子四时读书乐臂搁　清

高28、宽7厘米

BAMBOO ARM REST ENGRAVED WITH A PATTERN OF HAPPY READING, THE QING DYNASTY

Height: 28 cm, Width: 7 cm

臂搁浅刻远山近水，山窝草庐一人苦读，意境高远深邃。右上题曰："朱子四时读书乐大意，戊辰秋日，葆初珍赏"。

葆初（？～1900年），字效先，号冬心。崇绮子，世袭三等承恩公。工书、画。如此，戊辰当为清同治七年（1868年）。

The arm rest is shallow engraved with a pattern of landscape and a man studying hard in a mountain cottage. In addition, it features the inscriptions of "Happy reading of Zhu Zi in four seasons, Happy, Autumn of Year Wuchen, Baochu, Appreciation".

Bao Chu (? – 1900), with the literary name of Xiaoxian and courtesy name of Dongxin, was proficient in calligraphy and paintings. Year Wuchen refers to 1868, 7th year during Reign Tongzhi.

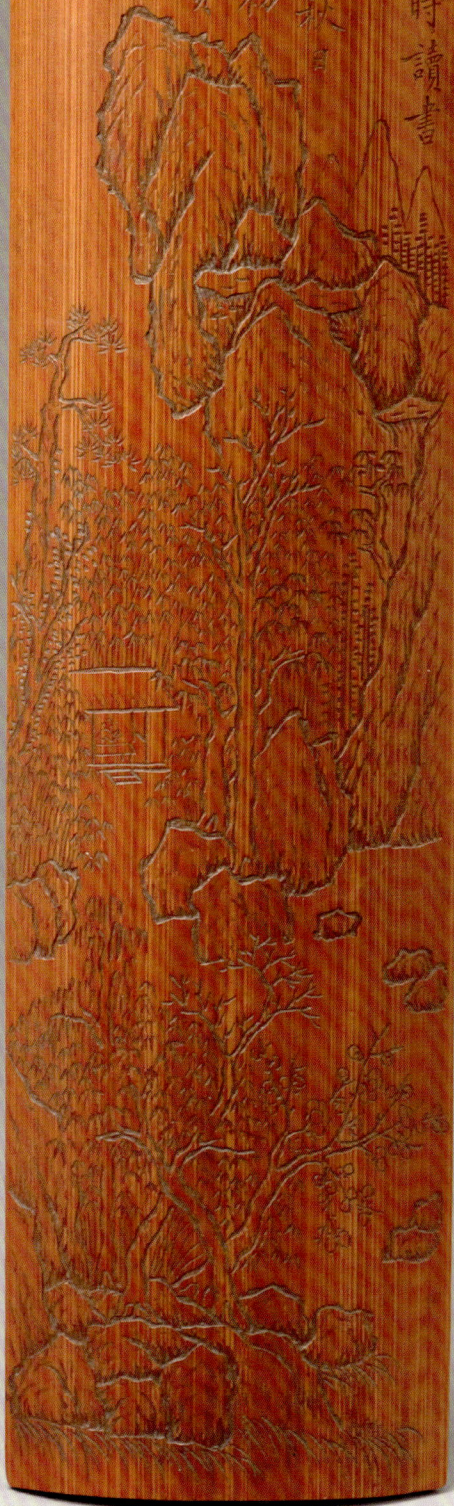

朱子四時讀書
樂大意
戊子秋日
森初
邗賀

**竹刻竹石纹臂搁**　清

长20、宽11.5厘米

BAMBOO ARM REST ENGRAVED WITH PATTERNS OF BAMBOOS AND STONES, THE QING DYNASTY

Length: 20 cm, Width: 11.5 cm

臂搁表面有顺着竹纹的细裂纹，浅刻竹石纹，石纹以短阴线表现，修竹随风轻舞，极具绘画功底。左上部题"清风嶰如"，落款"小泉"。

小泉，即邵玺，字廷玉，号小泉，清代青浦（今属上海市）人。国学生。花卉、人物宗黄慎。

The arm rest, with the crackle patterns along the texture of bamboo on the surface, features the bamboo and stone patterns in shallow engraving. The stone patterns are depicted in short intaglio lines and bamboos are dancing in the wind, which shows the painting skill of the creator. In addition, there are inscriptions of "Qingfeng Xieru" and "Xiaoquan" on the upper left.

Shao Xi, with the literary name of Tingyu and courtesy name of Xiaoquan, was born in Qingpu (Shanghai at present) in the Qing Dynasty. He was proficient in painting flowers and figures.

竹刻竹石纹臂搁　清

BAMBOO ARM REST ENGRAVED WITH PATTERNS OF BAMBOOS AND STONES, THE QING DYNASTY

## 竹刻清江独钓纹臂搁　清

长32.8厘米

BAMBOO ARM REST ENGRAVED WITH A PATTERN OF LONELY FISHING IN A CLEAR RIVER, THE QING DYNASTY

Length: 32.8 cm

臂搁皮色较深，浅刻山水纹，如芷岩一路风格。从题款看应是夏季山水景色。右上角题"甲辰夏日，步亭仁兄大人清玩，竹如写"。

竹如，即孙毓筠。名多琪，字竹如，安徽寿县人，秀才出身，优贡生，少年倜傥。清光绪三十年变卖家产在寿县北街僧格林沁祠旧址创办"蒙养学堂"，自任堂长。民国元年任安徽第一任都督。甲辰为光绪三十年（1904年），作品为清代末期。

The arm rest, with dark skin color, is shallow engraved with the landscape of summer and inscriptions of "Summer of year Jiachen, Buting Renxiong Daren, Qingwan, Zhu Ru, write".

Zhuru, referring to Sun Yujun with the courtesy name of Zhuru, was born in Shouxian. He was a successful candidate in the county-level imperial examination and he set up an elementary school in the original site of Sen Ge Lin Qin Ancestral Hall at the North Street of Shouxian by selling off his house and became the headmaster of the school in 30th year during Reign Guangxu. He became the first governor of Anhui in 1912. Year Jiachen refers to 1904, 30th year during Reign Guangxu.

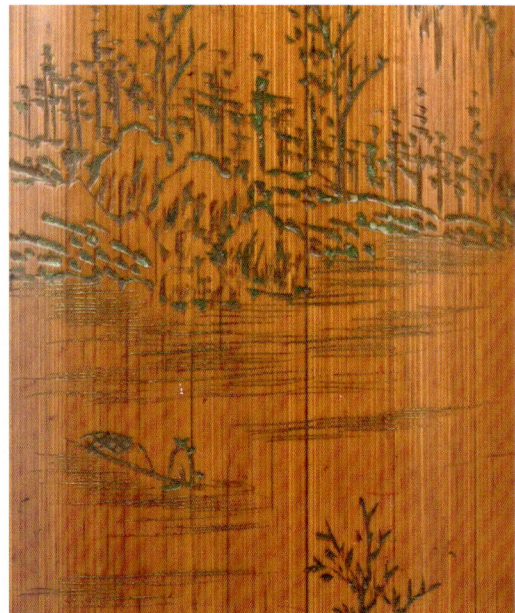

## 描银山水纹竹臂搁　清

长31.9厘米

SILVER-OUTLINED BAMBOO ARM REST WITH A PATTERN OF LANDSCAPE, THE QING DYNASTY

Length: 31.9 cm

此臂搁严格地说算不上竹刻，只不过材质是竹子。山水纹以银水描画，题款也以银水写就。不知是时间原因，还是银水调制不当，文字已模糊不清，勉强能看出后行为"皇甫仁兄大人法家正之"。

Strictly speaking, the arm rest is not a bamboo engraving, but an arm rest with bamboo as the material. The landscape painting is outlined in silver and the inscription is outlined in silver, too. However, either with the passage of times or with the improper silver, the characters are illegible. Vaguely seen are characters of "Huang Fu Ren Xiong Daren Fajia Zheng Zhi".

## 竹刻深秋野渡纹臂搁　清

长27.1厘米

BAMBOO ARM REST ENGRAVED WITH A PATTERN OF BOAT SAILING IN DEEP AUTUMN, THE QING DYNASTY

Length: 27.1 cm

臂搁皮色棕黄，浅刻深秋山水景色，一艘小船正满帆远航。右上角落款"子岩刻"。

子岩，似为方濬师（1830～1889），字子岩、子严，号梦簪，又号蕉轩。室名退一步斋。安徽定远人。咸丰举人。充通商衙门章京，擢广东道台，官至直隶永定河道。工书文。

The arm rest, with brownish yellow skin color, features the landscape in deep autumn with a boat setting sail. In addition, there is an inscription of "Engraved by Ziyan" on the upper right.

Fang Junshi (1830-1889), with the literary name of Ziyan, courtesy name of Mengzan, Jiaoxuan, was born in Dingyuan, Anhui. In addition, the pavilion he lived in was named "Pavilion of Standing Back". He was a successful candidate in the provincial-level imperial examination during Reign Xianfeng. He once took up different official posts in Guangdong and Zhili. He was also proficient in writing and calligraphy.

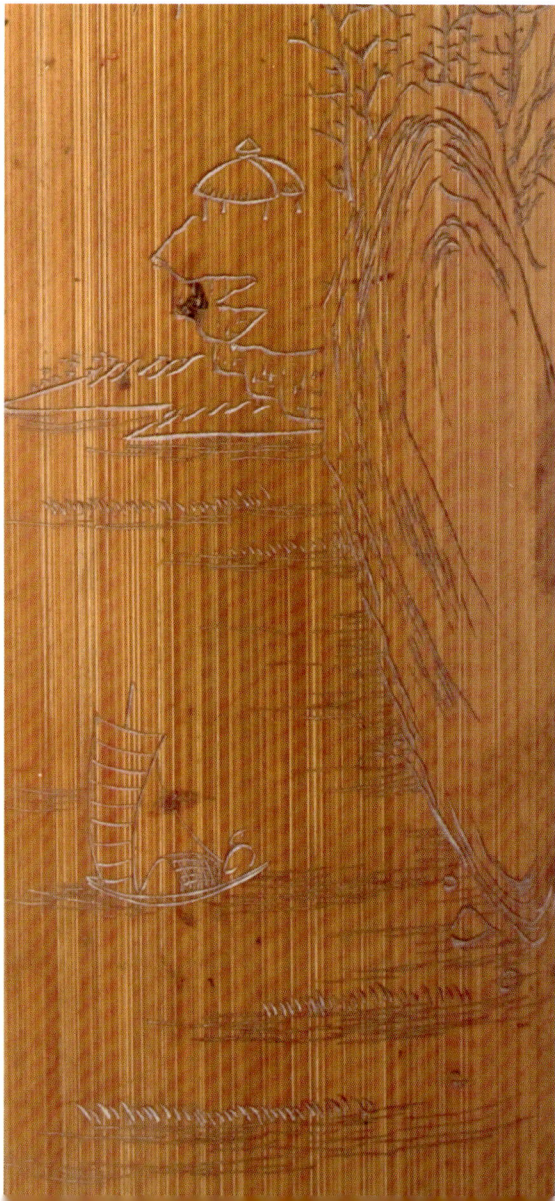

## 竹刻竹石纹臂搁　清

长28.3厘米

BAMBOO ARM REST ENGRAVED WITH PATTERNS OF BAMBOOS AND STONES, THE QING DYNASTY

Length: 28.3 cm

臂搁皮色红润，浅刻长有花草的山坡，坡上几杆修竹各呈姿态。左上角题"抚文与可笔法"，款"子文刻"。

子文，即周光煦（1851～1923年），字子文，亦作紫雯，浙江绍兴人。世业嫁妆木器店，幼习木器上花纹，邻有画师喜其有画才，教之书画。花卉、人物学萧山任氏，山水宗王原祁，兰竹花石宗郑燮，题画诗文亦效其体。

The arm rest, with ruddy skin color, is shallow engraved with a slope full of grass, flowers and slender bamboos. In addition, it features the inscriptions of "Fu Wen Yu Ke Bi Fa" and the seal of "Engraved by Ziwen" on the upper left.

Zhou Guangxu (1851-1923), with the literary name of Ziwen, was born in a family of wooden dowry articles in Shaoxing and learned pattern paintings on the wooden articles while young. He absorbed the styles of different schools: figure and flower painting from Ren in Xiaoshan, landscape painting from Wang Yuanqi, orchid, bamboo, flower and stone painting and poem composition from Zheng Xie.

竹刻竹石纹臂搁　清
BAMBOO ARM REST ENGRAVED WITH PATTERNS OF BAMBOOS AND STONES, THE QING DYNASTY

## 竹刻红拂女纹臂搁　民国

高30、宽9厘米

BAMBOO ARM REST ENGRAVED WITH A LADY CARRYING A WHISK, THE REPUBLIC OF CHINA

Height: 30 cm, Width: 9 cm

以细阴线刻画一持拂仕女，纹饰细腻，衣袂飘逸，大有吴带当风之势。臂搁上部题刻"乙酉新秋写应艺翁仁兄大人雅玩，少卿刘业昭"。

刘业昭（1910~2003年），字左彝，或曰少卿，湖南长沙人。国立杭州艺专毕业，受教于林风眠、潘天寿，曾往日本帝国美术学校暨日本明治大学研究。迁台后任"东南长官公署政务委员会"文化教育处处长，"交通部"司长等职，并任教于台湾艺专。善绘山水、花鸟、人物、翎毛走兽。乙酉为1945年，刘业昭35岁。

The arm rest features a lady carrying a whisk in fine intaglio lines. With minute patterns and elegant clothes, the lady is quite graceful and refined. Besides, on the upper is inscribed "Engraved in the autumn of year Yiyou, for the appreciation of Mr. Yiweng, Liu Yezhao, Shaoqing".

Liu Yezhao (1910-2003), with the literary names of Zuoyi and Shaoqing, was born in Changsha, Hunan. He graduated from Hangzhou Art College under the coach of Lin Fengmian and Pan Tianshou. Later, he studied in Meiji University in Japan. After moving to Taiwan, he became minister of Culture and Education of Political Commission, Southeast Government Office and director of Transport Department and at the same time, he taught in National Taiwan Art College. He was proficient in the paintings of landscape, birds, flowers, figures and beasts. Year Yiyou refers to 1945 when Liu Yezhao was 35 years old.

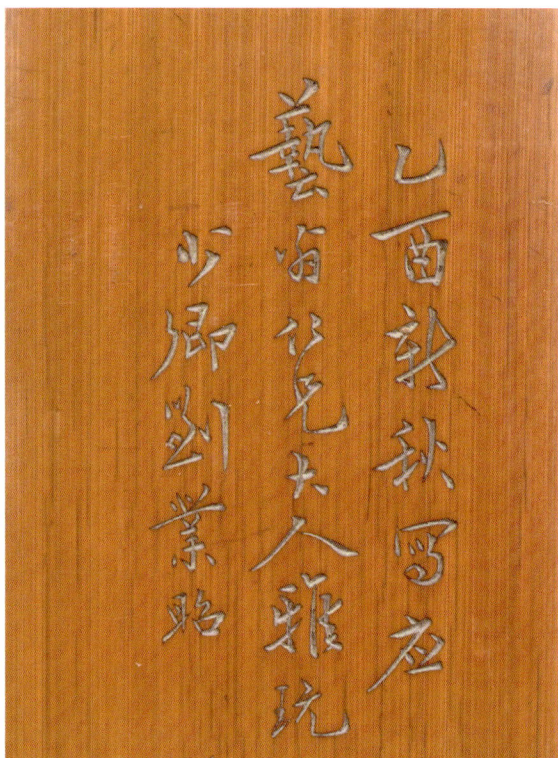

## 竹刻钟鼎文臂搁　民国

长32厘米

BAMBOO ARM REST ENGRAVED WITH BRONZE OBJECT CHARACTERS, THE REPUBLIC OF CHINA

Length: 32 cm

臂搁皮色红润，阴线刻古铜器铭文，落款"夏钟鼎文，甲寅梅月仿古，子安"，章"士俊"。

子安，即于子安，名士俊，江苏吴县人，光绪年间到北京以竹刻为业，擅长书法，自书自刻，其竹刻作品以行楷书为多，字迹娟秀，品种有扇骨、臂搁等。甲寅为民国四年（1914年）。

The arm rest, with ruddy skin color, is engraved with ancient bronze object inscriptions in intaglio lines and the inscriptions of "Bronze object characters, summer, ancient imitation in year Jiayin, Zi'an" and the seal of "Shijun".

Yu Zi'an, with another name of Shijun, was born in Wuxian, Jiangsu. During Reign Guangxu, he made a living by bamboo engraving in Beijing. In addition, he was proficient in calligraphy and bamboo engraving, in particular, of fine and elegant running and regular scripts on bamboo ribs and arm rests. Year Jiayin refers to 1914, 4th year during the Republic of China.

夏鐘鼎文

甲寅梅月仿古

子安

## 竹刻松鹤延年纹臂搁　现代

高24.5、宽7.2厘米

BAMBOO ARM REST ENGRAVED WITH PATTERNS OF PINES AND CRANES　THE MODERN TIMES

Height: 24.5 cm, Width: 7.2 cm

竹人以刀为笔，刻画松鹤图一幅，左上题七言诗句"鹤寿本来不足纪，苍官原是栋梁材"。落款"丁酉八月通夫画，介侯刻"。右下角阳文铭印"介侯七十后所作"。

介侯，即林兆禄（1887~1966年），字介侯。苏州人。擅刻竹，作品工雅，名载《竹人续录》。青年时代即喜研究金石文字，临池奏刀不辍。善于扇骨刻金石文字。久居上海，曾任上海文史馆馆员。丁酉为1957年，此时他正好七十高龄，与钤印相符。也许是老人自娱之作。

通夫，即蒋文达（生卒年不详），字成章，号通夫，别署剑猫。工书画，精篆刻。民国时客海上，颇负画名。

The arm rest features the patterns of pines and cranes, inscriptions of "Engraved by Jiehou in August 1957, the year Dingyou" on the upper left and the seal of "Engraved by Jiehou at the age of 70" cut in relief on the lower right corner.

Lin Zhaolu (1887-1966), with the literary name of Jiehou, was born in Suzhou and proficient in bamboo engraving. Due to his elegant works, his name is carried in *Records of Bamboo Engravers.* Since a young age, he was devoted to the studies of epigraphy, in particular, the epigraphy on fan ribs. He stayed in Shanghai for a long time in the Republic of China and was once the member of Shanghai Research Institute of Culture and History.

Jiang Wenda, with the literary name of Chengzhang, courtesy name of Tongfu, and pseudonym of Jianmao, was proficient in calligraphy, painting and seal engraving.

**竹刻博古集墨床**　清

长13.5厘米

BAMBOO INK REST, THE QING DYNASTY

Length: 13.5 cm

墨床皮色棕黄，为书卷状。刻"幽赏未巳"、"高谈转清"两方闲章。落款"蔚卿尊兄大人清玩，弟张韫山仿古"。张韫山，江苏兴化人，善雕刻，清光绪三年（1877年）曾在常州镌碑记"道南书院"事。

The ink rest, with brownish yellow skin color, shapes like a book engraved with two seals of "You Shang Wei Si" and "Gao Tan Zhuan Qing" and the inscriptions of "Engraved and donated by Zhang Yunshan to Revered Weiqing".

Zhang Yunshan, born in Xinghua, Jiangsu, was proficient in engraving and in 1877, 3rd year during Reign Guangxu of the Qing Dynasty, he engraved "Daonan Academy" in Changzhou.

## 竹刻"日形其短"铭墨床　清

长13.5、宽6.8厘米

BAMBOO INK REST, THE QING DYNASTY

Length: 13.5 cm, Width: 6.8 cm

墨床皮色棕红，为几案状，床面上下各两道凸棱线，中间阴文隶书"日形其短"，落款"拙斋作此以自警"。

拙斋，即贺雨亭（1873~1947年），字子云，号拙斋，山西柳林镇人。家学渊源，诗文俱佳。宣统元年，以优行廪生考中拔贡生，候补直隶州州判，授征仕郎。在任政绩颇佳，且热心教育，支持独子贺昌革命，1935年，时任红军总政治部副主任的贺昌在江西壮烈牺牲。

The ink rest, with brownish red skin color, shapes like a tea table with two convex lines on the surface and inscriptions of "Yue Xing Qi Duan" in intaglio official script in the center and inscriptions of "Engraved by Zhuozai for self-retrospection".

He Yuting (1873-1947), with the literary name of Ziyun and courtesy name of Zhuozai, was born in Liulin Town of Shanxi. Born in a family of learning, he was proficient in composing poems and essays. In the first year of Reign Xuantong, due to his good grades in the selection examination, he became official in Zhili state and achieved merits in his position. Besides, he was devoted to education and in supportive of his only son He Chang to take part in the revolutionary cause. Unfortunately, He Chang, deputy director of General Political Department sacrificed his life in Jiangxi in 1935.

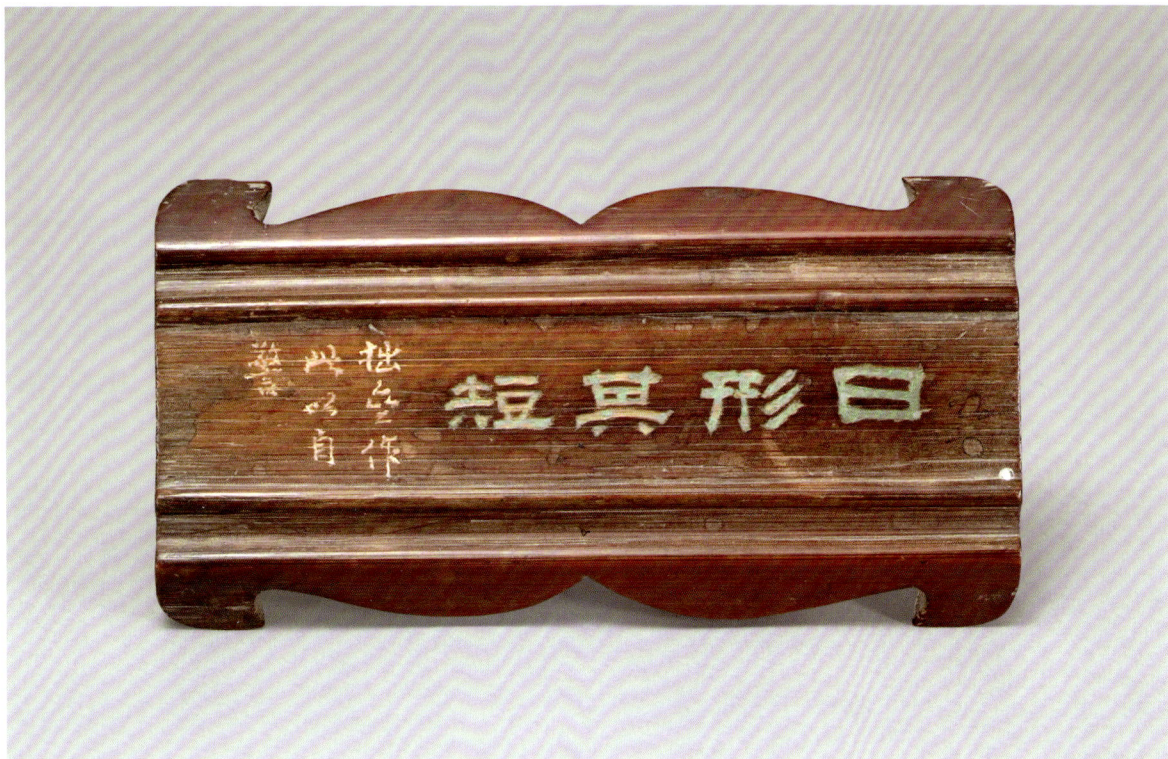

日形其短

槃以前
独坐作

## 竹刻行旅图小镇纸　清

高12、宽2厘米

BAMBOO PAPERWEIGHT ENGRAVED WITH A LONELY TRAVELER, THE QING DYNASTY

Height: 12 cm, Width: 2 cm

镇纸前面微弧，深棕色包浆，深雕一骑驴独行者在山间市镇中穿行。后面微凹，阴线刻月夜访友图。皮色虽不及前面深红，却有着古铜一般的色泽。镇纸前后的纹饰题材迥异，包浆深浅不一，有着转折变幻的意趣。

The paperweight, with a slight arch front and brown wrapping, features a lonely traveler on a donkey passing through a mountain town. Besides, the rear part is slightly concaved, engraved with a picture of visiting friends in the moonlight in intaglio. Though the skin color of the rear is not as red as the front, it shows the luster of copper. The front and rear parts are different in patterns and wrapping, showing an atmosphere of changing.